RESCUE FROM DISASTER

RESCUE FROM DISASTER

The History of the RFD Group

HAROLD NOCKOLDS

DAVID & CHARLES

Newton Abbot London North Pomfret (Vt)

British Library Cataloguing in Publication Data

Nockolds, Harold
  Rescue from disaster.
  1. RFD Group Limited
  I. Title
  338.7'62'086   HD9999.S9/

ISBN 0 7153 7969 0

Library of Congress Catalog Card Number 80-66422

Typeset by ABM Typographics Limited, Hull
Printed in Great Britain
by Redwood Burn Limited, Trowbridge and Esher
for David & Charles (Publishers) Limited
Brunel House Newton Abbot Devon

Published in the United States of America
by David & Charles Inc
North Pomfret Vermont 05053 USA

CONTENTS

FOREWORD

Most company histories are written to celebrate some particular anniversary. This is not true in our own case but we do feel we have recently passed a milestone where it is appropriate to look back for a moment to survey what has been built on the foundations laid by the individuals who started the various separate businesses which now form our family of companies, at a stage when we who are actively engaged in the Group are trying to strengthen and expand it and are reaching forward to new horizons.

There are a number of reasons for producing this book at this time. Firstly because we shall soon lose the first-hand contributions to the story which have been made by the personal recollections of individuals who were directly involved in the early days. Secondly because we believe that those now active will learn much for their own pleasure and advantage from the tale. Thirdly because as we widen our circle of customers, suppliers and other connections a book like this can more easily convey to them what sort of business they are dealing with. Finally and by no means least we think it is an interesting story in its own right: at a time when many thinking people in developed countries are increasingly coming to see from many different points of view the shortcomings of large corporations and the difficulties faced by State-owned industrial undertakings, it may be instructive to be reminded of the part played in economic affairs by the smaller companies and by individual human beings—whether they be the men of vision and determination who found a business, the managers who successfully carry on and develop it from these beginnings, or the more humble and anonymous majority whose skill and hard work achieve what others have seen was possible.

It is particularly easy for me to make this last claim because I am a relative newcomer to the Group as a non-executive director after thirty-five years of executive work elsewhere in much larger organisations. My own belief is that the concentration of industry in large corporations has been carried much too far in Britain for the health of the economy—with the blind acquiescence of all our political parties—with a consequent erosion of initiative and loss of vitality. These qualities which are so essential for the satisfaction of the customer's interest as well as the happiness of those who work in industry can more easily be fostered in an organisation which is large enough to maintain the economic strength necessary for survival and progress but not so large that the contribution that can be made by individuals is submerged. Such an organisation I believe RFD to be and such I hope it will always remain however successful it may be in the years ahead.

We feel we are fortunate to have secured the services of Harold Nockolds to tell our story, with his wide experience in the authorship of industrial histories. I hope the reader will find the tale with its many sub-plots an interesting one.

David Mynors
Chairman
RFD Group Limited
Godalming
February 1980

CHAPTER ONE

'GIVE THEM BOVRIL!'

When Reginald Dagnall walked into the entrance of the Air Ministry one day in 1920, his mood was a mixture of frustration and resignation. He was frustrated because in the post-war slump he had been unable to find another productive job after the airship and balloon factory he managed during the war closed down for lack of orders, and he was resigned to accepting a routine job in the Aeronautical Inspection Directorate. He was now on his way to the interview at which his AID appointment would be clinched.

At that moment he came face to face with a wartime acquaintance who worked for Short Brothers. When Dagnall told him what he was about to do, the acquaintance remarked that Shorts were looking for someone to supply them with rubberised pneumatic flotation bags to fit inside the fuselages of aeroplanes which they were making for the Royal Navy. These would provide extra buoyancy in the event of a forced landing in the sea. The order—worth £1,000—could be Dagnall's for the asking.

Dagnall did not hesitate to ask, and on the strength of that order—having narrowly avoided becoming a Man from the Ministry—he set up in business as the RFD Company, aeronautical engineers, at 21 Queen's Road, Hersham, near Walton-on-Thames, a few yards from the village green. His premises consisted of a two-storey Victorian stucco house with a shed behind. (After subsequently being used by various shopkeepers, the house is now occupied by a firm of solicitors, but there is an empty space where Dagnall's workshop once stood.)

It might be said that the RFD Group owes its existence to that chance encounter—a matter of seconds in timing—for who knows whether Reginald Dagnall, once enmeshed in the Civil Service, would have been able to break away? In fact, looking at his career up to that point, one is inclined to think that he would not have suffered the official life gladly and his strong individualism would have asserted itself before long.

9

To go back to the beginning, Reginald Foster Dagnall was born on 20 June 1888 at 'Brookfield', a tall terrace house at the end of Kempson Road where it abutted on to Eel Brook Common in the Fulham district of West London. The occupation of his father, Walter Dagnall, is given on his birth certificate as mat manufacturer. (In later years Dagnall used to describe his father, perhaps euphemistically, as a carpet manufacturer.) His mother was Frances Overton Brown before her marriage. 'Brookfield', with its three storeys, attics and basement (it still stands today) was entirely used as a residence, so Dagnall senior evidently carried on his business elsewhere—possibly in some buildings next door at the end of the terrace.

A few years later the family left Fulham and went to live at May Villa, Minerva Road, Kingston-on-Thames, a smaller detached house in a quiet cul-de-sac off The Fairfield. In due course Reggie was sent to Tiffin Boys' School, which had been opened in 1880. Tiffin's was a splendid new school with accommodation for 400 boys aged from ten to eighteen years, two science laboratories, a lecture room and a workshop. The school course led to matriculation, intermediate arts, science and engineering, and university scholarships. (Today Tiffin's—with 850 boys—is twice the size and is one of the few remaining grammar schools in the country. It has an exceptionally high success rate in preparing boys for Oxbridge examinations.)

Dagnall did not go to a university, and his first job was as a draughtsman at the Thames Iron Works and Shipbuilding Company at Bow Creek, Blackwall. This was in the days when the company was a pride of England in the heart of the flourishing Port of London. When Reginald Dagnall started work in the drawing office, the Thames Iron Works and Shipbuilding Company 'was capable of building and completely equipping, with the exception of the armament, the heaviest and largest class of warships that had up to that time been constructed in any shipyard in the United Kingdom' (*The Engineer*, 13 December 1894). Indeed, the Company had built HMS *Warrior*, the first sea-going ironclad in the world, in 1858–61 (now being renovated, 120 years later, by the Maritime Trust) and this had brought orders for similar warships from the Governments of Russia, Turkey, Germany, Spain, Portugal, Greece and Denmark, and with them a constant stream of distinguished visitors. From its yards the royal yacht *Fairy* was launched on the Thames. The ironworks side of the company was famous for its bridges—notably the Britannia vehicle bridge across the Menai Straits

10

and the Blackfriars railway bridge and Hammersmith bridge over the Thames—and it had made the iron roof of Alexandra Palace in London.

Notwithstanding this impressive record of achievement, the atmosphere of a great ironworks and shipyard did not appeal to young Reginald Dagnall. It was all too firmly established for his liking, and the very size of the company would not have suited his strong individualism. Whether he left the Thames Ironworks of his own accord or not is not recorded, but in 1908 he joined the engineering firm of D. Napier & Son at Acton. In 1895 the company had been bought from the executors of James Murdoch Napier by his youngest son, Montagu Stanley Napier, who was not in the company. Montagu Napier was then twenty-five and was soon looking for ways of adding to the long-established—but rather dull—business of making printing machinery and coin-classifying machines. He found fame, of course, with the Napier car and became one of the leaders of the growing motor industry in the Edwardian period. He also built a successful motor launch and in 1901 he offered for sale at £950 the Napier flying machine, a steerable balloon with an engine—in other words an airship.

Dagnall would have got to know about this project when he joined the company a few years later, and it is not too fanciful to think that it was the Napier flying machine that started his enthusiasm for airships. This would have led him to visit the International Aero and Marine Exhibitions held at Olympia in 1909 and 1910, at which the Willows airship was displayed. On 10 March 1910 Dagnall joined Willows as a mechanic. He was twenty-two years of age, and Willows was two years older. Why Dagnall left Napiers, a go-ahead company, to team up with Willows, an individual working on his own account, can only be guessed. With his uncompromising individualism he may have handed in his notice over some personal difference with his immediate boss—or he may have got the sack. Edwardian young men were notoriously restless, and to Dagnall the idea of working with Willows on his airship would have been a strong attraction.

As recorded by his biographer Ernest Willows had made his first airship in 1905, when he was nineteen, the cost being borne by his father. It was a small (12,500cu ft) non-rigid powered by a Peugeot motorcycle engine. Willows accomplished an 85-minute test flight on 5 September, keeping to the modest height of 120ft and spending most of the time manoeuvring with the aid of the airship's swivelling propellers.

11

Towards the end of 1909 Willows completed his second airship, the *Willows No 2*, which was a good deal bigger (21,000cu ft) and was fitted with a 30hp 8-cylinder air-cooled JAP engine. After local demonstration flights, including one from Cheltenham to Cardiff, he set out alone for London on 6 August 1910, reaching a height of 2,800ft at one point. Approaching his landing ground at the Crystal Palace, he ran out of petrol and lost his grapnel on a tree, drifting helplessly on to a forced landing at Lee, near Mottingham.

Willows' next objective was a flight from London to Paris. (The first cross-Channel flight had been made earlier in 1910 by Adolphe Bayard in the opposite direction.) Willows decided a larger airship was needed, so the *Willows No 3* was hurriedly constructed with an envelope of 30,000cu ft capacity. He also thought a companion was necessary, so he took with him a balloonist named Frank Gooden. Taking off from Wormwood Scrubs on the evening of 4 November 1910, *The City of Cardiff*, as the airship was now named, completed the Channel crossing according to plan—in spite of Gooden dropping their maps into the sea—but had to come down near Douai for repairs. A series of delays then intervened and it was not until 28 December that Willows arrived at the Issy-les-Moulineaux aerodrome just outside Paris.

When Willows next appeared with his airship, at the United Services Tournament at Bushey, near Watford, in March 1911, he was accompanied by his full-time mechanic, Reginald Dagnall. By this time Willows had decided to make his headquarters in the Midlands, first at Wolverhampton where he made many exhibition flights, and later at Birmingham. It was not long before Dagnall had learnt to handle the airship himself.

In May 1911 a company, E. T. Willows Limited, was formed with the principal object of making balloons and airships—they advertised a 4-seater airship built on the lines of *The City of Cardiff* for £900. They made and flew several balloons—one of them the 50,000cu ft *Alpha*, another called *Billie II*, and a smaller balloon referred to simply as 'the midget'. A contemporary newspaper report of the Birmingham Floral Fete at Handsworth describes how Dagnall took 'the midget' up in threatening weather at seven o'clock in the evening (it poured with rain later, during the firework display) and left the city following the Stratford Road. He came down near Studley and returned with his balloon in a milk float, arriving at the showground at three o'clock in the morning.

Willows also hoped to earn some ready cash by using *The City of Cardiff* as a flying advertisement hoarding. The company issued a brochure entitled 'Aerial Advertising', claiming sophisticated advantages for the banners with 10ft high lettering carried on the sides of the dirigible:

Sailing majestically overhead, with the world—so to speak—at its mercy, the airship provides the advertiser's *ideal solus position* . . .

Think of the effect on a thirsty crowd of trippers at Blackpool or Margate of the appearance of an airship carrying the magic name of a popular beer . . .

Similar psychological effects can be arranged. On a sweltering day in July an airship sailing over a jaded city, inviting the tired workers to a rest at a seaside resort, would have an immediate effect . . .

There is no question of circulation; no question of size or space; no question of position of hoarding—the advertisement is carried where all *must* see it.

Contracts for one or more flights on the same day ('no flight, no pay') were offered at £75 a day. Then came the most significant sentence from our point of view: '*The City of Cardiff* is now well equipped, and is in charge of an experienced pilot, Mr. R. F. Dagnall.'

It was probably during this period that the incident occurred which Dagnall recalled many years later in a newspaper interview:

Though I have been up in airships and balloons so many times, I have only had one adventure. With a mechanic I attempted an altitude record in an airship at Brooklands. It lost so much gas that it began to descend very rapidly. We jettisoned tools, coats, petrol, water, and everything else we could throw out, but we crashed nose first into a greenhouse. My only injury was a sprained ankle, which I got climbing down from a wall. I think that airships, properly handled, are safer even than aeroplanes.

During 1912 Dagnall worked with Willows on supplying and rigging a new envelope for the *Gamma* airship which had been made in 1910 by the Astra company of Paris for use by the Balloon Section of the British Army. The car had been made in England and the engine was initially an 80hp Green, which was later replaced by two Iris engines of 45hp each. The new envelope was 17ft longer than the original.

Willows' next airship was completed at Birmingham in the same year. With an envelope of only 20,000cu ft it was smaller than *The City of Cardiff* and was powered initially by a 20–24hp Vee-4-cylinder JAP engine which was later replaced by a 35hp 3-cylinder Anzani. After a favourable report by an airship pilot of the Royal Flying Corps, the *Willows No 4* was purchased by the Government before it had been flown and was sent to the Naval Wing of the RFC as a training airship. The price was £1,050 complete with shed.

In spite of these sales, E. T. Willows Limited had run out of money by the end of 1912 and Willows himself went bankrupt.

Reg Dagnall, now twenty-five years of age, found himself another job as assistant engineer with Spencer Brothers of Highbury, in North London, who had manufactured balloons and airships for many years. They had recently built a small non-rigid airship and had negotiated a contract with Benson's, the big advertising agency, who had persuaded the makers of Bovril, one of their most important clients, to use the airship for advertising their famous meat extract. Spencers were looking for an experienced pilot, and Dagnall was just the man for the job.

The Bovril airship was 96ft long and had a capacity of 40,000cu ft. To fill it with hydrogen cost £50 a time—400 gas cylinders, each weighing 1 cwt, were required. The airship was powered by a 40hp Green engine driving twin propellers by chains at 600 revolutions a minute. The framework of the car, which was almost as long as the envelope, was made of wood with open sides and looked rather like a chicken run when it was resting on the ground. 'Give Him Bovril' was painted in huge letters on the starboard side of the envelope and 'Give Her Bovril' to port.

Dagnall, sitting forward (immediately behind the engine), and his assistant, Sidney Heath, sitting aft (near the neck of the envelope), set off from Hendon for the Midlands on a rather misty day in October 1913. After reaching a height of 4,700ft Dagnall decided to come down to make sure where he was and finally landed for the night in a field on Sunderland Farm, Biggleswade. After a few days' delay in getting a further supply of hydrogen, he set off again, heading towards Peterborough. A reporter from the local paper wrote: 'The weather was brilliantly fine, with hardly any wind—a perfect flying day—and the airship ascended rapidly to a height of about a thousand feet, the propellers humming gaily as they cut the air.'

In fact it was far from being a perfect flying day, as the *Cambridge Daily News* reported the next day: 'When the pilots decided to effect a landing, it was found impossible to bring the machine to earth . . . It was

14

not until within six miles of Cambridge that they were at length able to come to ground.'

The reality was much more spectacular—indeed it was horrific—and there were times when people who actually saw it must have thought that the airship, apparently completely out of control as it slewed round crazily in wild circles, soaring to a great height and plunging down again, was bound to crash in the end. But Reginald Dagnall, calling on his long experience of airships, retained overall control of the situation, as he explained in a letter to the *Biggleswade Chronicle*:

The trouble was caused chiefly through the envelope being exposed to the sun, which warmed the gas and gave it more buoyancy. Consequently the airship rose to a considerable height; sometimes it rushed up from 500 feet to over 4,000 feet and down again as quickly. The sun and the height caused the gas to expand and compelled me to let out a large quantity to avoid the bag exploding. After a while the sun would disappear behind a cloud, the gas would then get chilled very quickly, losing its buoyancy, and cause the airship to come down with a rush, the gusty wind helped it on its downward path and turned it round and round. At one time near Cambridge the ship did three complete turns in 1½ minutes. To check these spasmodic occurrences and save damaging buildings etc., and incidentally our lives, I had to throw overboard 20 to 50 lb of sand to make the ship rise again. As soon as this was done, the sun would come out from behind the clouds and a repetition of the above would take place.

During the 50 miles which we covered, six of these 'stunts' occurred, which made it impossible to land in a small field; hence my reason for making for Ely, where there is plenty of open country. A safe landing was effected after three or four nasty bumps with mother earth, and I abandoned my flight to Wolverhampton via Peterborough.

Yours faithfully,
R. F. Dagnall

Cranfield,
Sandy Lane,
Hampton Wick, London.

In the early summer of 1914 Willows (who, in spite of being bankrupt, had somehow managed to build another airship, the *Willows No 5*) asked Dagnall to join him once more, this time in a new company he had joined called Airships Limited. In his capacity of chief engineer he

15

had been told to recruit an experienced staff, and he gave Dagnall the job of works manager at the company's factory at Merton, in South London. The premises had been built as a roller-skating rink before the war and the large floor area was ideal for making small airships and balloons. (After the war roller-skating went out of fashion and the building became the Wimbledon Palais de Danse.) One of the first machinists Dagnall took on was a bright young girl named Grace Turner, who had worked for a short time after leaving school at a neighbouring factory making electrically heated flying suits—aeroplanes had open cockpits in those days. (Mrs Dobson, as she was to become, was to stay with Dagnall and the RFD company for the rest of her working life, rising to the position of production manageress, and we shall hear more about her valuable work later.)

The founder of Airships Limited was George Holt Thomas, a man of remarkable vision and energy who is almost forgotten today but who was regarded by C. G. Grey, the redoubtable editor of *The Aeroplane*, as the true pioneer of British air transport and commercial aviation generally. In 1909 Holt Thomas had brought over the French pilot Louis Paulhan with his Henri Farman biplane to compete in the *Daily Mail* £10,000 race from London to Manchester. But first he persuaded Mr and Mrs Locke King to allow Paulhan to give a demonstration flight at their new Brooklands motor course in Surrey. They agreed that Major (later Colonel) Lindsay Lloyd, the clerk of the course, should have a space in the middle cleared for this purpose, and Paulhan gave his exhibition before an admiring crowd on 29 October 1909. Years later, C. G. Grey wrote: 'The name of George Holt Thomas deserves to be remembered as the founder of Brooklands aerodrome.' In 1911 Holt Thomas secured the British agency for Farman aeroplanes and Gnome aero-engines from France, and formed the Aircraft Manufacturing Company at Hendon. After the Great War it was Holt Thomas who started the first British airline with a service from London (Hounslow) to Paris, the inaugural flight being made on 25 August 1919. The service was run by Aircraft Transport & Travel, a subsidiary of the Aircraft Manufacturing Company.

Airships Limited was formed by Holt Thomas in February 1914 as a subsidiary of the Aircraft Manufacturing Company. Its first activity was to acquire the British manufacturing rights of the Astra-Torres airships made in Paris. Two 350,000cu ft airships of this type were supplied to the Admiralty before the war broke out and they were used as escorts for the transports which carried the British Expeditionary Force across the Channel to France in August and September 1914.

The sinking of HMS *Formidable* by a German submarine off the Isle of Wight in the New Year with the loss of 547 lives brought home to the Admiralty the insecurity of the Channel and coast. To seek out intruding U-boats the Royal Navy had only five airships. On 28 February 1915 Lord Fisher, the First Sea Lord, called a meeting of senior naval officers and others (including Holt Thomas) at which he outlined his plan to have a fleet of small, fast airships to operate as anti-submarine patrols. Instructions to produce prototypes were given to the Naval Wing of the Royal Flying Corps and two private firms, Armstrong Whitworth and Airships Limited.

The Royal Navy team got to work immediately. Working to a plan claimed to have been mulled over in the mess at Farnborough a few months earlier, they produced their prototype in three weeks by adapting the fuselage of a BE 2c aeroplane so that it could be slung below the envelope of the *Willows No 4* airship that had been used for training and was lying deflated in a shed at Farnborough.

The first airship submitted by Airships Limited, which was delivered to the RNAS station at Kingsnorth in Kent in March, was rejected because Willows refused to comply with the specification, which was for a simple airship that could be made quickly and cheaply and flown by relatively inexperienced crews. Instead, he insisted on producing a large and complicated ship of 70,000cu ft capacity powered by a 100hp Curtis engine with his pet swivelling propellers (which actually worked very well). Moreover he would agree to only very slight modifications being made to it. This wasn't good enough for the Admiralty, so Airships Limited were sent back to square one. Taking a leaf out of the Navy's book, they produced a simpler airship with a car that was based on the fuselage of the Maurice Farman aeroplane, and this was accepted. Dagnall took part in the testing of both these airships.

Armstrong Whitworth, after some initial difficulties, turned in an airship very much like the Navy one, and this too was passed by the Admiralty.

All three types went into production. The Armstrong Whitworth had a 12-hour advantage in high-speed endurance over the Royal Navy's BE 2c model, while the Airships Limited type was a bit slower than both but made up for it by being more comfortable for the crew. Thus was born the SS airship (variously interpreted as Sea Scout,

Submarine Spotter and Submarine Searcher) which was to become popularly known as the Blimp. About 150 SS airships of various types were made during the war and did splendid work on anti-submarine patrols. They were later supplemented by Coastal Patrol, Coastal, and Coastal Star airships with a longer range, for which Airships Limited supplied larger envelopes of Astra-Torres design.

In July 1916 Willows parted company with Holt Thomas and took a job as an assistant inspector for the rapidly growing Aeronautical Inspection Department of the Air Ministry. (A few months before the war ended Willows returned to industry for a short time, trading as the Willows Aircraft Company and manufacturing a small number of observation balloons for the Government in a converted roller-skating rink at Cardiff. He was killed in 1926 in an accident to the captive balloon in which he was giving passenger ascents at a Bedford flower show.)

Willows' departure left Dagnall in charge of Airships Limited as general manager of the company. After making a batch of SS airships, the Merton factory concentrated on the production of captive observation balloons which were used by the Army for artillery spotting and by the Royal Navy for submarine detection by ships at sea. The yellowing prints in a photograph album kept by Dagnall at the time show that they started making the first British-built German Drachen kite balloons in 1915 and tested them at the Kite Balloon Training Wing at Roehampton. SS airships and Drachen kite balloons could be built simultaneously in the spacious factory. After several intermediate types of the Drachen had been produced it was replaced by the improved French version called the Caquot, which was also made in various types and became the standard observation balloon used by the Army and Royal Navy for the rest of the war.

As the manager of Airships Limited, Dagnall was sent over to France several times to advise the Army on the handling and maintenance of captive observation balloons, the first time in September 1915, the second in May 1916, and again in April 1917 when he carried a special request from the Military Aeronautics Directorate to the Military Landing Officer at Southampton for his embarkation to be facilitated as much as possible on account of the 'very urgent' nature of his duties. Finally in September 1917 he went to Paris 'on urgent Admiralty business'.

Airships Limited also made the air ballonets which enabled the airships and balloons to retain their shape as the gas expanded and contracted. 'Nurse' balloons for use in conjunction with the ballonets were also made. The nurse balloon allowed the ballonet to be deflated when the balloon or airship was 'bagged' on the ground or deck, and the main balloon to be kept full of gas. A silk model kite balloon for seaplane wireless is seen under construction in 1917, and other special types made were 3,500cu ft weather balloons and a 1,000cu ft expanding panel balloon. Various experimental models were made towards the end of the war, and the last photograph in the album illustrates a fabric tent for housing tanks.

The fabric for the balloons was supplied by several cotton mills working to Government contracts. One of the names Dagnall noticed on the bales as they arrived at Merton was the Perseverance Mill Company of Padiham in Lancashire. Although he was to do business with this company after the war, as we shall see, Dagnall was never to know that one day Perseverance Mill would become a major member of the RFD Group—an event that did not occur until long after his death.

Altogether, more than 1,000 kite balloon envelopes and suspensions were made during the war by Airships Limited, who became the largest individual makers of kite balloons in the country. Satellite factories at Balham and Wandsworth were started to supplement the output of Merton. The workforce numbered over 1,000 skilled fabric workers (mostly women) and riggers. The planes, rudders and car structures for the airships (including engine and propeller installations) and the basket-work cars for the balloons were made in a separate factory at Hendon, also under Dagnall's control, where there was an experimental labora-tory for testing materials and parts and a 7ft wind tunnel for testing scale models of the airships and balloons.

Shortly before the end of the war Dagnall made up some experi-mental inflatable boats (presumably to fulfil a Government development contract) and took them along to Wisley Lake near Guildford to try them out. From the rather misty photographs taken on the occasion, it seems that three of them were single-seater canoes and the fourth was a raft that could hold four people. Paddles and/or a sail were used to propel them.

Dagnall was by no means the pioneer of the inflatable raft. Rafts supported by inflated animal skins were used by Alexander the Great for exploring the Upper Ganges, but it was not until Charles Mackin-tosh patented his rubberised cloth in 1843 that the modern type of inflatable became possible, first for ferrying troops and later in the form of pontoons. There was then a gap in the development of inflatables until Dagnall's experiments on Wisley Lake in 1919.

After the Armistice on 11 November 1918, all Government contracts were immediately cancelled and Airships Limited—in common with hundreds of other companies wholly engaged on war work—faced a bleak outlook. Holt Thomas planned a campaign to interest prospective civilian customers in the merits of the airship, pointing out in a catalogue that British airships had spent more than 80,000 hours in the air during the war (50,000 of them in the ten months of 1918) and had travelled about 2.3 million miles. Among the uses for airships he envisaged were police supervision in remote countries, fishing protection duties, marine salvage work, surveying and prospecting, the delivery of post and newspapers, passenger transport in places where speed was not a decisive factor, and private ownership in the form of an air yacht. Specifications and illustrations of four types of aircraft and an observation balloon, all based on wartime designs, were given in the catalogue, and the company offered to make airships to meet any special requirements.

A few months before the war ended Dagnall had written an article on 'The Future of Airships' in the Sunday, 24 March 1918 issue of *Reynold's Newspaper*. (This was the week-end of the final German offensive and Reuter's special correspondent commented on the front page: 'The greatest struggle in the world's history is now deciding the world's future.') Dagnall's personal opinion about airships savoured of optimism —'I would say that the airship has a future, but its present activities are limited, more so than those of the aeroplane.' The airship, he thought, would develop on three lines—'a medium-size rigid that will be used as the eyes of the Navy, a very large super-rigid for commercial work, cargo carrying and passengers, and a small non-rigid for light commercial work, joy-riding and training'. He became somewhat starry-eyed perhaps when he added: 'I look forward with considerable interest to the time when big West End stores will be employing airships for the delivery of parcels to different parts of the country.' He went on: 'When I was flying the "Bovril" airship some time ago, I had a similar scheme mapped out, but unfortunately the war interfered with it.' But no one was interested in airships, except the Services, and they were making their own. Curiously, the inflatable dinghy, which was to play such a big part in Dagnall's future, does not seem to have been developed any further by Airships Limited, but an attempt was made to market the 'Camel' or salvage pontoon for raising sunken ships. The Camel was a large cylinder about 8ft in diameter made of specially prepared canvas and was completely air- and water-tight. The requisite number of pontoons were taken down under water in a deflated state and placed in the hold or secured to the side of the sunken ship before being inflated from above. The Camel was supplied in various sizes and was claimed to give an upward lift of from 25 to 100 tons when inflated. The company also advertised water ballast bags for ships which occupied a very small space when packed up and not in use. But neither of these devices could keep the company afloat.

And so we come to the point when Airships Limited became completely deflated and was wound up in 1920. Just before this melancholy event, Dagnall took to the air once more. Accompanied by Lieutenant Onishi of the Japanese Imperial Navy, he made the first balloon ascent from Mitcham gasworks in South London on 5 February 1920. After passing over the Airship Limited factory at Merton, the balloon was lost to sight when it entered cloud at a height of 5,100ft over Putney. When Dagnall descended he found himself over Ealing with Northolt aerodrome ahead. The balloonists landed there safely and were given 'a fine time' by the RAF officers in the mess.

A year before, Dagnall had written a little book entitled *Ballooning*, in a series covering sporting pastimes ranging from *Dog Breaking* to *Camping Out* and *The Cultivation of the Common Hare*. In it he described the technique of ascending and descending through cloud (without the help of modern navigational aids) at the same height as the cloud he encountered over Putney:

> We find out exactly where we are by our map before going into the cloud, and make sure we are not too near the sea or any place where landing cannot be made. The balloon not having enough buoyancy will not penetrate it, so a little more sand (about half a bag for a 60,000 cu ft balloon) is thrown over. We now enter the cloud, which is very similar to a damp mist. The upward run of the balloon is here impeded owing to the moisture settling on the envelope and making it slightly heavy.
>
> Assuming we have passed through the cloud, the sun will be shining on the balloon and will dry off the moisture. We now sail along on or above the cloud for, say, half an hour, and decide to descend to find our whereabouts. The neck lines are now adjusted as previously stated. If

the cloud is fairly dense, the balloon will simply bump it and ascend again until it finds a less dense spot, unless, of course, the buoyancy of the balloon has dropped considerably. When it has found the weak spot in the cloud it will descend. We may find that the balloon will not penetrate the cloud when it is desired to descend. In this case a sharp pull at the valve cord will release some of the gas and decrease the buoyancy and so enable it to descend. This practice is not recommended but may be used as a last resource when there is grave doubt as to the balloon being too near the coast or too near some dangerous place.

When descension through cloud has been made, our first operation after bringing the balloon to its equilibrium is to find out over what part of the country we are. Therefore we glance around and see if it is possible to discern a river, railway or fairly large town, taking into account that whilst above the clouds the wind might have been in another direction. If you cannot locate your position fairly quickly, make absolutely sure the sea is not ahead. If satisfied, ascertain the quantity of ballast or sand left. If not more than two bags, pick a fairly large field and land. Assuming we have three or four bags left, it will be quite safe to continue the journey under these circumstances. We ascertain our whereabouts, and should this be impossible owing to lack of land marks, we come down low and shout to the people below, asking for the name of the nearest large town, then ascend again and find the place on the map.

With little or no interest being shown in the things he really wanted to make or do, and unable to find an opportunity to use the managerial skills he had developed during the war, Reginald Dagnall was forced to consider becoming something he had always rather despised, a civil servant—escaping at the last minute, as we have seen, to start in business on his own account at the age of thirty-two.

CHAPTER TWO

FROM DOUGHNUTS TO DINGHIES

For the material he required to make the flotation bags for Short Brothers, Dagnall naturally turned to a company he had known as a major supplier of balloon fabric during the war. But although he knew the reputation of the Perseverance Mill, they knew nothing about him. Their wartime contracts had come from the Air Ministry and the fabric had been sent via the proofing company to Airships Limited. So when the RFD enquiry landed on the desk of Alan Noble, Perseverance Mill's sales manager, in 1920, the name meant nothing to him. He showed it to his father, Herbert, the chairman, who was equally in the dark.

'You'd better go and have a look at the place and see what it's all about,' he said.

In due course Alan reported that the RFD Company consisted of a large tin hut and nothing much else. But he had met Dagnall and liked the look of him.

'Do you want to do business with him?' his father asked, and Alan replied 'Yes, I do.'

So began the RFD–Perseverance association that was to ripen till it became a full-blooded amalgamation nearly forty years later.

Fortunately for Dagnall, Short Brothers were not the only firm interested in salvaging their aeroplanes from the sea and during the next few years he received further orders from the Bristol Aeroplane Company, Blackburn Aircraft, Fairey Aviation, H. H. Martyn & Company, the Hawker Engineering Company and others for flotation bags tailored to fit individual aircraft.

An advertisement postcard produced by Dagnall at this time states that while specialising in emergency flotation gear for aeroplanes, 'the RFD Company also undertakes every description of rope, wire, canvas and fabric work, balloons, etc, etc.' Drawing on his brief experience with inflatable boats during the war, he started to produce collapsible

23

inflatable boats made of 3-ply rubberised fabric which could be rolled up and packed away in a very small space.

By 1926 the business was more than the little workshop at Hersham could cope with, so Dagnall decided to move to a garage at 17 Stoke Road, Guildford, which comprised a small two-storey building and a smaller single-storey shed behind, with a solitary hand-operated petrol pump in the forecourt. He continued to run the garage as a sideline to begin with, while he carried on his real business of making up flotation bags in the building at the rear, but it was allowed to peter out after a time. He and his wife Ada moved into a house next door. His staff consisted of about a dozen girls (the number changed according to the orders in hand) under the supervision of Grace Dobson and one man, a fitter. Dagnall did much of the production work himself.

The primary purpose of flotation gear was to give the aircraft a better chance of being salvaged. The fact that this also improved the prospect of the crew being picked up was incidental at this stage. Ditching an aircraft in those days was hazardous for the crew because the fixed undercarriage tended to flip the aeroplane upside down as it hit the water. It was hoped they would survive by extricating themselves from the upturned machine and climbing on top to await rescue. If the pilot succeeded in landing without overturning, the crew sat in the aircraft which, being a biplane and of wooden construction, floated quite well anyway. With flotation gear fitted, it could stay on the surface for a considerable time.

The first flotation bags were installed inside the fuselage in series and were held in position by straps. Before the aeroplane took off they were inflated by means of an ordinary pump. A vent to atmosphere allowed for expansion and contraction of the air in climbing and descending. If the pilot had to come down on the sea he closed the vent and sealed the bags by turning a cock.

In some of the aircraft produced in the late 1920s there was no space in which atmospheric flotation bags could be stowed; in others there was room only in the tail of the machine, though buoyancy was also needed at the forward end. In both cases the requirement could be met by stowing deflated bags behind panels which could be burst off when the bags were inflated. This required the use of a compressed air bottle with a valve connected by a chain and sprocket mechanism to a hand wheel operated by the pilot as the aeroplane came to rest on the water.

By 1929 RFD had supplied some 1,200 flotation bags, mostly for aircraft flying from carriers and therefore liable to finish up in the sea on landing or taking off.

In spite of his preoccupation with flotation gear, Dagnall pressed on with the development of the RFD inflatable boat for pleasure purposes, particularly fishing and duck-shooting. He took out a patent for certain features and in 1929 produced a catalogue of the improved version. The standard boat (a larger one could be supplied) measured 10ft by 4ft by 2ft and had a pointed bow and broad stern. Together with a pair of sculls its price was £16. A transom was provided for fitting an outboard motor. Dagnall showed his ingenuity by making the boat really portable—complete with floorboards, bow-post, rowlocks (spelt 'rollocks' in the catalogue), seats and lifelines, it could be rolled up in a valise measuring 2ft x 1ft 3in x 9in and weighed only 55lb. The boat could be inflated by hand bellows or by using the exhaust from a car or motor-cycle, which took about three minutes. A tube from the valise, which acted as an inflation bag, was fitted to the exhaust pipe by a conical connector and two more tubes were connected to nozzles in the boat. The engine was then started up, slowly at first, until the valise was full. Gently revving up the engine raised the pressure evenly in the boat and the engine was kept going until the boat was almost drum tight (about 2psi). The boat could be 'topped up' with a pump when required. A typical Dagnall touch in the brochure stated: 'When turned upside down the boat makes a splendid diving-board. Right way up, a bed complete with pillow, or a bath.' Production of the RFD portable boat continued until 1933.

Meanwhile in 1928 some publicity was given to the fact that an inflatable boat was being carried on each of the four Supermarine Southampton flying boats taking part in the Services cruise to the Far East (believed to be the first recorded instance of the use of inflatable dinghies by the RAF). The experimental dinghy, triangular in shape and stowed under the pilot's seat, was made by the Royal Aircraft Establishment allegedly from a French design. It was used for ferrying between the aircraft and the shore, and had the great advantage over a normal dinghy that it could not damage the hull of the flying boat when bumping alongside.

It seemed odd to many people at the time that, considering his reputation and experience, Dagnall did not supply these early dinghies. C. Howarth, the Air Ministry official who was later responsible for development work on inflatable dinghies and who knew Dagnall well, was probably right when he guessed that the reason lay in differences of opinion between Dagnall and the Ministry on points of design.

After the Far East cruise, small rubber C-type triangular dinghies went into regular service with RAF flying boats and seaplanes, principally for ferry work between the aircraft and the shore. The initial contract was believed to have gone to Siebe, Gorman & Company, the makers of diving equipment, who exhibited collapsible dinghies at the aircraft exhibitions in 1929 and 1930.

In the late twenties and early thirties the development of flotation gear became linked with that of inflatable dinghies. This process began with the decision of the Air Ministry that military aircraft mainly of wooden construction could no longer be sanctioned as British first-line military aircraft. The result was a change in aircraft design and construction from wooden-framed biplanes with fixed undercarriage to all-metal monoplanes with retractable undercarriage. RFD were involved in one of the first machines of the new type, the Fairey long-range monoplane produced in 1929 for an attempt on the duration flight from England to Africa, for which they supplied a range of flotation bags.

Aircraft of metal construction had lower inherent buoyancy than the wooden biplane, bringing about a change in flotation-gear technique. In some cases it was possible to stow two inflatable bags—one on the port side and the other on the starboard side of the fuselage near the pilot's cockpit, but this was not practicable on the new IIIF aircraft made by the Fairey Aviation Company, who specialised in aircraft for the Fleet Air Arm. The chief designer, Marcel Lobelle, suggested that a deflated balloon should be fitted in the centre of the main plane, stowed in a blow-out compartment so that when the aircraft descended on water the balloon could be inflated and would support the aircraft, to which it could be attached by a system of wires. Lobelle discussed his idea with Group Captain H. R. Busteed who was working on Fleet Air Arm matters for the Government and was the originator of the flotation bag. Busteed improved on the suggestion by proposing that a large circular lifebelt would be preferable to a balloon. At this point Lobelle and Busteed were joined in their discussions by Robert Youngman, the Air Ministry's resident technical officer at Fairey Aviation, who made the further suggestion that the lifebelt—or 'doughnut ring'—should be constructed with a floor so that the crew could be accommodated in it until they were rescued. Thus two purposes would be served—salvaging the aircraft and saving the crew—by combining the flotation gear and a rubber dinghy in one piece of equipment. Or so it seemed at the time.

Rather to Lobelle's surprise, Youngman took out a patent for the complete circular dinghy/flotation gear and this was accepted in July 1932. In the meantime Lobelle had placed an order with RFD for five dinghies, which were delivered to Fairey Aviation in September. (In June RFD had executed their first order for dinghies for the aircraft industry when they supplied thirty of a Ministry pattern to Reid & Sigrist, the aeronautical instrument firm who also made hand and foot bellows for dinghies.)

During 1933 Dagnall produced a series of prototype Youngman dinghies of 1,900lb, 3,000lb and 4,500lb buoyancy for Fairey Aviation. The drawings supplied gave little more than the general arrangement of the dinghies with internal and external measurements, and the detailed development work on the buoyancy tubes, floor and the selection of materials was entrusted to Dagnall. In October RFD began direct development work for the Air Ministry.

But the Youngman dinghy could not be regarded as the answer to salvaging ditched aircraft without some form of automatic inflation. Once the aircraft had landed on the sea it was essential that the whole apparatus should operate instantaneously and with the greatest possible certainty, bearing in mind any damage or injury that might be sustained by the aircraft and its occupants. The non-automatic inflation of flotation gear already described (consisting of a chain-and-sprocket system operated by the pilot by means of a hand wheel) was cumbersome, slow, uncertain and vulnerable. A few years earlier, in June 1930, the Walter Kidde Company Inc of New York, USA, who were specialists in fire-fighting equipment, had patented the Lux automatic head for automatically inflating dinghies by the release of liquid carbon dioxide from a cylinder which was converted to a gaseous state on exposure to the air. This was done by means of hydrostatic valves which, when immersed in about two feet of water, built up pressure in a tube. This pressure was transmitted to a pneumatic head in which a piston was driven forward to pierce the sealing disc on the carbon dioxide cylinder, thus permitting the discharge of the gas into the inflatable bag. The head could also be operated manually by a wheel rotating on a screw thread to force down the cutting mechanism; a degree of remote control was achieved by pulling a wire which operated the wheel, but the direction of pull had to be from a fixed point, which restricted the location of the dinghy in its stowage. The whole system was submitted to the Air Ministry in 1932 through the company's British subsidiary, the Walter Kidde Company Limited of Northolt in Middlesex.

Dagnall was aware of the need for automatic inflation and set about improving upon the method devised by the American company. In November 1932 he applied for a patent to cover his solution, in which automatic operation of the head was effected by the incorporation of an electric circuit broken by an immersion switch (a pair of spacer plates) located on the lowest convenient point on the aircraft. When they were immersed in water the spacer plates completed the circuit, allowing the current to pass and explode a cartridge in the head. The combustion gases generated by the cartridge drove a piston to which was attached a cutter blade, and this pierced the frangible sealing disc on the gas container. Manual operation was accomplished by pulling a cable which caused a cam to rotate, forcing down the piston and cutter mechanism. The Dagnall cam method had the edge over the Walter Kidde system in that the cable could be pulled from any direction, which enabled all aircraft to be equipped with dinghies regardless of whether they were designed to carry them or not. This was to prove particularly valuable a few years later during the war when American civil aircraft designed for overland flights were put to military use involving sea crossings.

In the patent Dagnall was jointly named as the inventor with Alan H. Reffel who, according to Dagnall, worked up his original idea. They had first met through their mutual interest in gliding. (In 1934 Reffel assigned his whole rights to Dagnall. He had previously invented a robot-man which moved and spoke and was exhibited in London stores and in the United States.) A minor improvement, a detent lever which prevented the cutter from being forced by the pressure of the escaping gas into a position in which it impeded the flow of the gas, was covered by a later patent in which Dagnall was joined by James G. Lambert, who had worked with him back in his draughtsman days at the Thames Iron Works. Lambert, a free-lance consulting engineer, had been employed in the first place to make drawings of the Dagnall–Reffel head and in the course of doing so had put forward suggestions for improvements. (Dagnall later on purchased Lambert's rights too.)

The Air Ministry began by telling the Walter Kidde people that they were not interested in their proposal, but they quickly changed their minds. During April and May 1933 trials were held with aircraft working in conjunction with HMS *Ark Royal*, equipped with prototype Youngman circular dinghies, Walter Kidde automatic inflation equipment, and a buoyancy bag (presumably made by RFD) in the rear of the fuselage. Fourteen trials took place—three at Chatham, five at Portsmouth, and six at sea. All but two were successful. In the very first trial, held at Chatham at the end of April, the Lux inflation head failed to operate completely when the aeroplane (one of the three prototype Fairey Queens) was lowered into the water in an inverted position over the side of the ship. The aeroplane was hauled out of the water and on examination it was found that the gas cylinder outlet was frozen up. As this was the result of the aeroplane having just completed a six-hour flotation test, the inflation equipment could hardly be blamed.

The second failure occurred at sea on 2 May and unhappily resulted in the loss of the same aeroplane. When it was lowered over the side and was partly submerged it was noticed that the Lux automatic head had failed to function. At that moment, by an unfortunate coincidence, the quick-release coupling on the crane purchase was accidentally tripped and the aircraft rapidly disappeared from sight beneath the waves, carrying away the 100ft cable and buoy which was attached to the salvage slings. The failure of the inflation equipment was thought to be due to an accumulation of water in the pipeline after ditching, thus creating an artificial head which destroyed the effectiveness of the system. Such a failure would not have happened in normal service conditions and the Lux automatic head and method of inflation were considered satisfactory.

In one of the twelve successful tests a Hawker Nimrod (the sea-going version of the Hawker Fury) was deliberately ditched in flight alongside the *Ark Royal*. The aircraft was equipped with two flotation bags let in the underside of the wings near the root and covered by blow-out panels. The Nimrod was flown into the sea in a semi-stalled attitude and turned a somersault directly the wheels hit the water. The automatic head operated immediately and the flotation bags were inflated before the pilot was clear of the aircraft. In spite of the pilot's foot fouling the rudder-bar strop, which momentarily delayed his exit from the cockpit, the interval of time between the cockpit becoming submerged and the surfacing of the pilot was only six seconds. The aircraft was then left in the water to complete a six-hour flotation test, at the end of which its position was almost unchanged.

As a result of these trials the Ministry decided to adopt all the equipment. About a dozen Lux inflation heads were imported from Walter Kidde in the United States and fitted to dinghies carried by Hawker Harts while arrangements were made by the British company to manufacture the heads using some American-made parts, including spindles and castings for the housing. RFD were given the contract to make the Youngman dinghies and Dagnall put forward his own method of inflating them by his cartridge-operated head. However he was turned down by the Ministry and the Walter Kidde fire-extinguisher-type Lux head went into service. (But that was not to be the end of the story, as we shall see.)

Dagnall started delivery of his first production order for twenty-one Youngman E-type (3,000lb buoyancy) dinghies to Fairey Aviation for the IIIF in March 1934. Deliveries of the F-type (1,900lb) dinghy for smaller aircraft like the Hawker Osprey followed shortly afterwards. A larger model, the G-type (4,500lb), was supplied in 1935 for such aircraft as the Fairey Swordfish. In 1934 RFD were licensed by Youngman to produce the dinghy commercially on the basis of a $7\frac{1}{2}$ per cent royalty. (Youngman had by this time left the Air Ministry and was chief engineer of Fairey Aviation.)

Dagnall found he needed more money to finance this new dinghy business so in 1934 he turned RFD into a private limited company. The additional money was put up by local people.

The Youngman dinghy turned out to have only a limited use as a combined flotation gear and dinghy, as was noted in the minutes of a meeting of the technical sub-committee, Fleet Air Arm–Advisory Committee on Aircraft, held on 7 July 1933:

> It was stated that in anything but calm sea conditions, it would be impossible for the crew to remain in the dinghy if at the same time the aircraft is attached to it. The continual revolving movement of the dinghy, first in one direction and then in the other, and also the sea washing over it, would make it impossible for the crew to remain for any length of time.
>
> It was pointed out by the DTD that the dinghy was provided as a salvage scheme for aircraft when a forced landing is made on a Carrier and the aircraft goes overboard. In these cases it is only necessary for the aircraft and crew to be kept afloat for a short time. When, however, a

forced landing is made at sea away from shipping, the dinghy could be immediately slipped from the aircraft. After further discussion it was decided that the dinghy should be slipped immediately the aircraft landed on the water, except in the case of a machine going over the side of a Carrier when other means of rescue would be readily available.

By 1936 the policy of salvaging ditched aircraft was being closely re-examined. It was found to be a very expensive business stripping a ditched aircraft down, cleaning and re-assembling it, while experience showed that the aircraft generally suffered extensive damage in ditching and further damage when it was hauled out of the water. (Usually the tail was the only visible part of the aircraft, and aircraft were not made to be lifted by the tail alone).

During the summer and autumn of that year extensive sea trials were carried out which confirmed conclusively the drawbacks of the Youngman dinghy in its dual-purpose form. The Air Ministry there-upon made two important decisions: that the dinghies should not be attached to the aircraft, which would henceforth be free to sink, and that the dinghies should be for the rescue of the crew only. This meant that the Youngman combined flotation gear–rescue dinghy was no longer required, and production was finally discontinued in 1938. During the five years since its introduction, RFD had made 691 Youngman dinghies, for which they were paid £22,771.

But though the Youngman dinghy failed in its original dual-purpose form, it was a milestone in inflatable history because its circular shape set the pattern of most aviation and marine liferafts of the future.

So long as the circular dinghy was attached to the top of the aircraft by shroud wires it had been a fairly stable platform for the crew to climb aboard from the water, but without the wires it was a very different story. It was found that when the first man attempted to do so, the dinghy more often than not overturned on top of him.

Mr Howarth of the Air Ministry made two suggestions, neither of which was successful. The first was that the buoyancy tube surrounding the dinghy should be waisted at the boarding point, which lowered the freeboard. Apart from the fact that this allowed the water to enter the dinghy at the boarding point, the idea did not work because the two butt ends of the buoyancy chamber acted like jaws and converged on the body of the person attempting to enter the dinghy. The second proposal was that entry should be effected through a trap door in the floor of the dinghy. This was rejected because crew members who were

31

either injured or non-swimmers would not be able to reach the trap door.

It was left to the RFD works manager, Charles Fellowes, to produce the answer. (Fellowes had been with Dagnall since the Willows days, following him to Airships Limited and eventually becoming technical manager.) His suggestion was that ballast bags in the form of water pockets should be fitted to the underside of the dinghy. These ballast bags were of sufficient size to prevent the dinghy from overturning, and rope ladders and a handline were provided to enable the crew to haul themselves aboard. A lifeline was also fitted round the periphery of the dinghy to which survivors could cling until their turn came to clamber in. A tug on a trip line passing from the lifeline to the water pockets caused them to collapse and eject the water they contained, so that they could be emptied at will.

These modifications were incorporated in production models early in 1937 and Howarth, for the Air Ministry, acknowledged the considerable help he had received from the company. Dagnall had attended all the trials and carried out modifications quickly and at short notice.

The Youngman 1,900lb buoyancy F-type dinghy became known as the H-type dinghy Mark I; the 3,000lb buoyancy Youngman E-type was renamed the J-type dinghy Mark I; and the 4,500lb buoyancy G-type Youngman dinghy became obsolete because such a buoyancy was not required to support the crew alone. In the Mark III versions of the H-type and J-type dinghies the diameter of the buoyancy tubes was reduced (without affecting the buoyancy) and the floor was lowered to accommodate crews of five and seven respectively.

Up to 1938 all circular dinghies supplied to the Air Ministry were made by RFD, but when the H-type and J-type dinghies went into full production at Guildford that year a contract was also given to the Dunlop Rubber Company. By the outbreak of war in 1939 all the aircraft in Coastal Command and Bomber Command (Stirlings, Manchesters, Halifaxes and Wellingtons) were equipped with 5-man and 7-man dinghies. Incidentally, aircraft dinghies were constructed in a dark brown proofed material until 1938, when it was decided to adopt a pigmentation of 'traffic yellow' in the proofing to assist their identification at sea.

The Air Ministry decision to abandon ditched aircraft also affected the policy of carrying any form of flotation gear. From that time onwards flotation bags were carried in only a few aircraft, notably the

In 1913 Reginald Dagnall, by then an experienced pilot, was hired by Spencer Brothers to fly one of their airships to advertise Bovril. In the close-up picture he can be seen at the controls sitting in the skeleton fuselage behind a 40 h.p. Green engine and two chain-driven propellers. It was in these primitive conditions that Dagnall and his assistant, Sidney Heath, survived the perilous flight from Biggleswade to Ely described in the text

Reginald Dagnall: (*right*) a snapshot taken in his office at the Merton factory of Airships Limited in June 1918. On his desk-top can be seen a model of the Blimp anti-submarine patrol airship produced by the company before it went over to the manufacture of observation balloons for the rest of World War I

(*below*) While managing the observation balloon factories of Airships Limited in 1918, Reginald Dagnall (extreme right) made some experimental inflatable boats and tried them out on Wisley Lake, near Ripley in Surrey

Swordfish, the Warwick and the Wellington. The Wellington had such bad ditching qualities that without the bags, which were carried in the bomb bays, the crew would not have had sufficient time to escape before the aircraft sank.

Ever since 1932, when he patented his cartridge-operated inflation head, Dagnall had persevered in his attempts to convince the Air Ministry of its superiority over the Walter Kidde pneumatic head which they had preferred. He demonstrated the head to Ministry officials on numerous occasions—at Gosport (where he gave at least six demonstrations in 1936), Farnborough, Fairey Aviation, Vickers and Hawkers, but he made no progress until both the Ministry and Walter Kidde began to get worried about the number of accidents that were occurring to aircraft which could be attributed to the pneumatic head. In several cases the head operated of its own accord while the aircraft was in flight, with the result that the inflated dinghy became entangled in the controls of the machine and made it crash. The trouble arose mostly with Fleet Air Arm aircraft with folding wings in which the dinghy was stowed in the top main plane and was connected by a rubber tube to the hydrostatic switch. It was possible to nip this tube in unfolding the wings, with the result that when the aircraft reached a certain altitude the trapped air expanded and actuated the head. There were several other defects as well, but that was the main one.

Eventually the Walter Kidde Company were compelled to approach Dagnall and ask if they could manufacture cartridge-operated heads under his patents. Dagnall agreed and in May 1937 an exclusive licence agreement was concluded between the two companies by which RFD were to receive a royalty of 10 per cent on the selling price of explosion-operated heads and 5 per cent on cam-operated heads manufactured by Walter Kidde. The royalty on Government orders would be negotiable, with a minimum of 5 per cent. Walter Kidde designed the heads for mass production (Dagnall had made only prototypes), obtained the approval of the Air Ministry, and started production in 1938. The equipment finally adopted by the Royal Air Force combined some features of the Dagnall patents with others that were contributed by the Walter Kidde Company.

Before we continue our narrative, let us turn back for the space of a chapter to see what other activities Dagnall was engaged in as the pause between two world wars came to an end.

CHAPTER THREE

DAGNALL TO THE RESCUE

Flotation gear and inflatable dinghies, although the major part of RFD's business, were not the only things that concerned Dagnall as the twenties gave way to the thirties.

The first was a return to his early connection with airships, for which he retained a lasting affection. (The logotype he designed for the letters RFD in the title of his company was in the shape of an airship and the letters themselves exactly copied the style used in the logotype of Airships Limited.) In 1929, when the big R.100 and R.101 rigid airships were launched for the Air Minstry at Howden and Cardington, a private firm called the Airship Development Company made a small non-rigid airship (a second followed later) on the lines of the wartime Blimp with the old idea of letting advertising space on the envelope. This was the first privately built airship in Britain since the *Willows No 5* in 1913. Knowing Dagnall's experience of this kind of work, both in making Blimps at Airships Limited and with flying advertising airships for Ernest Willows and Spencer before the war, they commissioned the RFD Company to make the envelope, which was 140ft long and 30ft in diameter in the middle. The 320 separate panels were made of 2-ply rubberised fabric coated with aluminium to protect it from the sun, double stitched, lapped, taped and cemented with 15cwt of rubber solution. Inside the envelope were two ballonets which were used to maintain the pressure and trim the ship. The whole envelope entailed more than six miles of stitching. It cost £200 to inflate it with hydrogen. To begin with, a 75hp air-cooled ABC Hornet engine (curiously enough made at Hersham) was used, but this was replaced later by a DH Gipsy engine.

The AD1 airship was built at Cramlington in Northumberland in a shed constructed in 1918 for NS airships but never used for its original purpose. It underwent its first flight trials on 18 September 1929 and the next morning the *Daily Mail* carried a report by Major

F. M. Dougall which admirably conveyed the style and spirit of the times:

> Captain McColl, cool and smiling, took one cockpit. I perched myself somewhat insecurely behind him. The engine roared to life . . .
>
> 'Let go all!' We are off.
>
> 'Airshipping', next to ballooning, is the most delightful form of travel. It has not the perfect silence of the balloon, but at any rate you know where you are going and are not at the mercy of chance winds.
>
> The ground drops away below, the landing party dwindle to the size of ants. To the south a haze of smoke shows where Newcastle lies. Far to the east another haze betokens the 'grey North Sea'. We throttle down, and now it is possible to talk in comfort. 'Isn't it topping?' asked McColl, pleased as a schoolboy that this ship, the child of his brain, really works. He struggled against so many adversities to bring to fruit this idea of his.
>
> 'Topping,' I reply. 'Let's go to Holland.'

The AD1 episode forged another link between RFD and the Perseverance Mill, which supplied the fabric for the envelope. This was described by *Flight* as being 'of a special kind with particularly low permeability and great strength'. (Perseverance Mill's dominant position as the makers of fabric for airships in the United States as well as in Britain is recounted in Chapter Eight.)

Another reminder of the old days at Merton came in 1929 when RFD received an order from the Air Ministry for six R-type observation balloons together with three accompanying nurse balloons. This gave rise to some bitter exchanges between Dagnall and the AID inspector, who rejected the whole batch to begin with, and there was a long drawn-out argument before the order was completed. Having produced more than a thousand observation balloons during the war, Dagnall was entitled to think that he knew more about making them than did a mere civil servant. No wonder he was angry . . . (His reputation with the Air Ministry as the authority on making kite balloons was to be fully vindicated a few years later, as we shall see.)

In the same year a 'one-off' order for a small balloon brought the company the unusual distinction of being praised in a letter to *The Times,* a newspaper not normally given to publicising individual companies in its lofty correspondence columns. It read:

TRIBUTE TO AN ENGLISH FIRM
To the Editor of *The Times*

Sir,—You may think that the following example of promptitude in manufacturing goods in England and in delivering them overseas deserves to be put on record in your columns, particularly since the article supplied was a somewhat unusual one.

I use a small balloon for taking air photographs of the archaeological excavations here. My old one came to an untimely end a few weeks ago; so, on November 25 I cabled to the R.F.D. Company, of Guildford, a firm with which I had not previously dealt, asking them to make me a new one to a particular specification, and on the following day I confirmed my cable by letter in which I asked that the balloon might be sent to me by the shortest route.

A balloon is not altogether an easy thing to plan or put together, but mine was completed and despatched via Imperial Airways on December 7, reaching Gaza on the 13th. Only four days later—on the 17th—I received it at Haifa, and one must remember that during this interval it had been in two Custom Houses, and that the distance between Gaza and Haifa is quite 120 miles. I might even have hastened the time of delivery by going to Gaza and clearing it at the Custom House there, but I did not do so, and the total number of days which elapsed between the giving of the order and the receipt of the goods thus stands at the very respectable figure of 22.

Yours faithfully,
P. L. O. GUY

The University of Chicago, Megiddo Expedition,
  Megiddo, Palestine, Dec. 18

Dagnall's interest in flying and flying machines had so far been confined to balloons and airships. The flotation gear was no more than an ingenious adjunct to the aeroplane using inflation techniques that were familiar to him, and he never seems to have been attracted by aeroplanes themselves. However, when gliding was revived on a large scale in 1930 (there had been upsurges in 1911 and again in 1922, but they had petered out), Dagnall responded immediately and was soon in the thick of the movement. He was one of the original directors of the British Gliding Association along with Colonel the Master of Sempill, the chairman, E. C. Gordon England and L. Howard Flanders.

What everyone wanted was a preliminary training glider, and Dagnall provided it by building a machine (at his own expense) for the BGA based on the design of the German Zögling glider, a popular type for beginners at the Wasserkuppe school in the Rhon, which had six of them. The plans of the Zögling had been obtained by *The Aeroplane* from the National Gliding Association of America and were passed on to the BGA so that a primary glider of proven design could be made available to the dozen British gliding clubs that had already been formed. Dagnall replaced the original wooden fuselage members (except the A-frame) of the Zögling with steel tubes, which did away with some of the bracing wires and strengthened the support of the tail structure.

In the 12 March 1930 issue of *The Aeroplane* the following advertisement appeared:

> The RFD company begs to announce that they are now in a position to accept orders for gliders and sailplanes of types approved by the BGA. Orders will be accepted in strict rotation.

Dagnall organised the first informal meeting of the London Gliding Club at Stoke Park Farm, Guildford, close to his little factory in Stoke Road. The purpose was to evaluate the 'Dagling', as his glider was dubbed, against an example of the Zögling, which Dagnall had imported from Germany and presented to the BGA. Germany, of course, was considered to be more advanced in gliding than most countries, largely on account of the ban on aeroplane construction after the war. Nevertheless, the Dagling proved to be more popular than the German glider among the well-known aviation people who tried both types during the afternoon, and it cost only £45—£35 less than the Zögling. It had to be admitted however that nothing very conclusive—apart from trim and controllability—could be ascertained in the short hops permitted by the almost level ground. Then everyone adjourned to the nearby Caxton Hotel where Dagnall entertained them to tea.

Assured of the supply of training gliders from Guildford, gliding clubs rapidly increased in number until by May 1931 there were forty-five of them throughout the British Isles—many using RFD machines. For a time Dagnall attended the meetings of the London Gliding Club at Ivinghoe Beacon (near the village of Dagnall!) before they found a permanent home at Dunstable, by which time he had become chairman of the Surrey Gliding Club, first at Chilworth, not far from Guildford, and later at Meonstoke near Winchester, where he engineered the merging of the club with two others in the Southdown Gliding Club. *Flight* reported that in the first year 'Freddie', the Surrey club's RFD glider, was launched over 300 times, 'which figure speaks well for the quality of the machine and for the care and repair work of the riggers'. With his usual generosity, Dagnall provided workshop facilities for the club at Guildford.

As an aviator himself, it was to be expected that Reg Dagnall would try his hand at gliding. He was one of the first to fly the Dagling at Stoke Park and *The Aeroplane* commented 'That its path was somewhat erratic is not surprising as Mr. Dagnall had never flown a heavier-than-air craft before.' Later he had another go at Rottingdean which ended in the glider dropping like a stone from a height of about 30ft. He was shaken but unhurt, while his wife Ada, having a quiet cup of tea in the marquee with her young nephew, Frank Martin, had a terrible fright when the cry went up 'Dagnall's crashed!'

The RFD sailplane, nicknamed 'Daniel', was designed by Dagnall's assistant, J. Bewsher, and completed its flight trials at Brighton on 7–8 March 1931, an event that was celebrated by a dinner at Ye Angel Hotel, Guildford, a few days later. Its price was fixed at £190, but only the prototype was made. Captain A. N. Stratton, the Surrey Gliding Club's instructor, demonstrated the sailplane in various parts of the country, and at the Surrey Club's Whitsun meeting in 1931 at Rotting-dean A. H. Reffel set up a duration record of 1hr 40min in it. In the following month Dagnall entered it for Stratton to fly in the *Daily Mail* £1,000 competition for the first double crossing of the English Channel, being the only entrant to have his machine launched from a balloon at a height of 10,000ft. RFD also built a sailplane to the order of the designer, C. H. Latimer-Needham, who called it the Albatross. Only one was made. J. N. Rickard, who is now the senior assistant road safety officer of the City of Westminster, spent all his spare time as a lad hanging round Dagnall and his gliders, and recalls that the silver-and-blue Albatross—considered very advanced for its day—was the first sailplane he saw that could fly along the Ivinghoe ridge and back again without landing. Rickard later learnt to fly an RFD primary glider when the club moved to Dunstable.

In January 1932 RFD announced that they were giving up making gliders because of the pressure of work they were doing for the Air Ministry. (RFD's work on inflatable dinghies was just beginning.) By that time the Guildford factory had produced twenty-seven primary gliders.

Dagnall resigned from the board of directors of the British Gliding Association but carried on for several years as chairman of the Southdown Gliding Club. The name RFD continued to be associated with gliding, however, through the sale of complete sets of plans and working drawings of the RFD primary glider by the BGA for the princely sum of £2. The result was that they were made by a number of firms—Dart, Dunstable, Abbott-Baynes, Slingsby and Hawkridge— and all primary gliders were popularly called Daglings.

No sooner had he withdrawn from the gliding scene than Dagnall found himself involved in yet another form of non-powered flight. Dr William Mercer, who for many years was Dagnall's general practitioner and personal friend—he also became the RFD company doctor —has told me how Dagnall was always making notes on the backs of envelopes and scraps of paper as new ideas to be followed up later occurred to him while he was talking or reading. It was probably something he read in *The Aeroplane* that moved him to investigate a project for making parachutes by two partners, Raymond Quilter and James Gregory, who were having difficulty in finding financial backing. So one morning in 1932 Dagnall rang the number where Quilter was to be found—it was in fact the Quilter stockbroking firm in the City—and an appointment was made for him to meet Raymond at a flat in Davies Street, Mayfair, belonging to his father Sir Cuthbert Quilter. Before we see what happened at that meeting, a glance at the background will help to put the people concerned into perspective.

Dagnall's telephone call was answered by Arthur Dickinson, who had an office in the stockbrokers' premises but was not actually a member of the firm. Dickinson (who was to become managing director of the GQ Parachute Company in time) had qualified as an accountant in his birthplace, Wigan, in 1924. In 1931, seeing no future in his home town in those black years of depression, he applied for and got the job of secretary to the trustees of the Quilter estate in East Anglia, working from the stockbroking office in Gresham Street. The estate had been built up at the end of the last century by Raymond's grandfather, whose father, William Quilter, had come up to London from Walton in Suffolk as an accountant/stockbroker and in 1870 founded the Association of Accountants, the forerunner of the present Institute of Chartered Accountants. On ethical grounds he had to concentrate on the accountancy side of his work so he transferred the stockbroking business to his son, William Cuthbert Quilter, who made so much money (largely out of floating foreign railways and the National Telephone Company) that he was able to return to his family grass roots in Suffolk to build up an estate at Bawdsey Manor until it covered 12,000 acres in the area east of Ipswich between the river Deben and the North Sea. He was MP for Sudbury from 1885 to 1906 and was created a baronet in 1897. He died in 1911, leaving more than a million pounds to his eldest son, William Eley Cuthbert, the second baronet and father of Raymond. (A younger son, Roger Quilter, was the composer of much charming music, notably settings of Shakespeare and other poets for voice and piano.)

John Raymond Cuthbert Quilter was born in 1902. Although his father went to Harrow, Raymond—like his Uncle Roger—was sent to Eton, which he hated. There was apparently no question of his going to a university (his father had been to Cambridge) and as the second son of the family Raymond seems to have been cast into limbo on leaving school. However he made good use of his freedom by spending most of his time with the fishermen at Great Yarmouth, going to sea with them and conceiving a plan to run a fleet of trawlers. Before this wayward ambition could crystallise into a bone of contention with his father, his elder brother George Eley died in 1919 and Raymond found himself the heir to the estate. He was now required to follow an orthodox career and on 15 March 1922 he was commissioned in the Grenadier Guards (in which his Uncle John had served as a major before being killed in action at the Dardanelles as lieutenant-colonel commanding the Hood Battalion of the Royal Naval Division). He attended an equitation course at Aldershot (which he passed) soon after joining, but to his independent spirit, corporate life was just as uncongenial in the Army as it had been at Eton.

What finally disillusioned him with the monotony of peacetime soldiering was when he overheard two elderly (every bit of forty) members of the Guards Club after lunch one day trying to make up their minds what on earth they could do to fill in the rest of the afternoon. 'My God,' he thought, 'I shall be like that one day, with absolutely nothing to do.' After over three and a half years' service he resigned his commission on 23 December 1925.

But he was no more contented when he was sent to work in the family stockbroking business, Indeed by now, for want of anything more satisfying to do, he had thrown himself with gusto into the carefree life of the 1920s. One of his extravaganzas was to start a band composed of street musicians, in which he himself played the guitar. He left the Stock Exchange after only a short stay, if not of his own accord at least without any regrets, and found himself back at Bawdsey Manor with time on his hands. He played golf (from scratch), indulged the enjoyment of shooting and fishing that he inherited from his father, took up archery with initial enthusiasm and considerable accuracy, cooked excellent meals, and became an accomplished photographer. He seems to have derived his restless spirit from his mother (before her marriage the Hon Gwynedd Douglas-Pennant, daughter of Lord Penrhyn) who, in the current phrase, was regarded as 'awfully go-ahead.' She was keen on everything that was new—she even invented things herself—and took up the very latest fashions.

Nevertheless, to those who knew him well, Raymond Quilter—for all his fits of boisterous exuberance—was really rather an unhappy person at this stage. He even went to Canada House one day with the intention of emigrating. At the last minute he tossed a coin—and it came down to stay in England.

Then one day in 1927 he went down to Brooklands to have a look at the first flying school that had just been opened there by Lieutenant-Colonel G. L. P. Henderson. He was taken up in one of the school's Avro biplanes and immediately decided to learn to fly. Towards the end of 1928 Henderson went back to his original premises at Croydon and the Brooklands school was taken over by his chief instructor, Captain Duncan Davis. According to R. Colston Shepherd, the air correspondent, Davis used to say that he had practically no money himself but he had some wealthy friends 'who helped him to buy a typewriter and three Avros'. Whether Raymond Quilter was one of those wealthy people or not, he certainly became a life-long friend of Duncan Davis, and he was one of his forty pupils who qualified for their A licences in 1929. By that time he had his own de Havilland Moth and in the six months after getting his licence he put in about one thousand hours. He thrived in the cheerful atmosphere of the flying school, and at the Brooklands Aero Club when it was formed in 1930.

In 1928 James Russell, one of the original American Army team working on parachute development at McCook airfield after the First World War, came over to England in the wake of Leslie Irvin, who had started a British subsidiary company two years earlier on the strength of a contract to supply the RAF with parachutes. Russell planned to set up a British company to manufacture his unique Russell 'Lobe' parachute, and to whip up support he engaged John Tranum, the remarkable Danish stunt man, to give a series of demonstration jumps, starting with one at Stag Lane aerodrome that may well have been witnessed by Quilter. Raymond was certainly present two years later when Tranum appeared at the opening flying meeting at Brooklands in March. Starting in fine style by being borne aloft in an aeroplane piloted by Duncan Davis himself, Tranum finished ignominiously by landing slap in the middle of the sewage farm adjoining the aerodrome.

By this time Raymond Quilter was convinced of the merits of the Russell 'Lobe' parachute. Not content with strapping one to his body whenever he flew, he made his first jump and was immediately 'hooked' on parachuting. Soon he was giving demonstration jumps at shows and meetings, including those of the Household Brigade Flying Club. (In his time he was to make well over a hundred jumps, many of them free-fall.) He got to know Tranum well and took him up in his aeroplane for one of his demonstrations.

With his practical enthusiasm for the Russell 'Lobe', Quilter enjoyed visiting the little factory at Stoke Newington and discussing problems of design and construction and parachuting technique with James Gregory, the works manager.

Gregory was one of the most experienced parachutists in the country, having served in the Royal Flying Corps and the Royal Air Force from 1917 to 1923, during which he spent three and a half years in the parachute test section at Martlesham. He was then employed by Calthrop Aerial Patents, makers of the Guardian Angel parachute, from 1923 to 1929, when he joined Russell. For Quilter this contact with Gregory was crucial. All of a sudden he found himself with a sense of purpose, he knew what he wanted to do—not merely for pleasure, but as a worthwhile job. They agreed to go into partnership together in making an improved parachute, and in 1931 Gregory left the British Russell company and joined Quilter.

They had nothing to go on but their aspirations and enthusiasm—no funds, no office, no formal business arrangement. An obvious source of money was Sir Cuthbert, but Raymond decided that a direct approach would not succeed. Instead, he sought the help of Sir Cuthbert's new financial adviser, Arthur Dickinson, who had recently taken up his post as secretary to the Quilter trustees. Both aged about thirty, they understood each other well and their different qualities and personalities were complementary. Dickinson persuaded Sir Cuthbert to open his purse strings to a very limited degree, just enough to buy parachute fabric and pay the partners' working expenses—under Dickinson's financial supervision.

Raymond did his best to interest his father in the project, as C. G. Grey, editor of *The Aeroplane* and a staunch supporter, described in a later article:

> I have a vivid memory of seeing him in a big shed at Brooklands demonstrating the operation and comfort of his parachute harness to his father by tricing that august gentleman up in it and hauling him on a block and tackle into the roof among the girders and letting him gently down again. It was an awe-inspiring sight.

It was on this restricted basis that Raymond Quilter and James Gregory, calling themselves the GQ Parachute Company, rubbed along for the next year, taking the Irving and Russell parachutes as their model and designing an improved type that conformed with Air Ministry specifications and at the same time was cheap enough to be bought by private fliers. The first few prototypes were stitched by Gregory's wife on her sewing machine in their tenement flat in Peabody Buildings near Holborn.

Then in 1932 Reginald Dagnall appeared on the scene and met Quilter and Dickinson in Sir Cuthbert Quilter's flat. Dickinson recalls that Dagnall and Quilter 'got on like a house on fire'. This instant recognition of a kindred spirit, creating a frank and trusting understanding, seems to have been a characteristic of both men. Dagnall, on hearing that the partners had no works in which to make parachutes, offered them space on the first floor of his factory at Guildford and the use of a couple of girl operators with their sewing machines—all free of charge.

'It was always known as the Greenhouse because it was all glass— boiling hot in summer and freezing cold in winter', as Lady Quilter remembers it. But there the GQ Parachute Company found a 'works' of its own at last, on terms that Dickinson could never have hoped for.

This *ad hoc* arrangement continued until the spring of 1934, when it was realised that it ought to be put on a proper basis. So Dickinson formed a private company, the GQ Parachute Company Limited, with authorised capital of £2,000, 760 fully paid-up shares being allotted to Quilter, 555 to Dagnall, and 10 to Dickinson. These three comprised the board of directors, their fees being £50 a year. Gregory did not join the board, but was paid a salary of £5 a week plus a bonus of 10 per cent of the net profits. He also received, jointly with Quilter, a royalty of 2½ per cent on the sale price of all parachutes sold. It was agreed that Dagnall should be paid—for the first time—a rent of £80 a year for the use of the factory.

Raymond Quilter took the opportunity to bring in Captain Gerald Dean as a consultant to advise the company on developing parachute sales to South America, for which he was paid the handsome fee of 10 guineas a year. Dean had valuable connections there through his wife, Olive, who had a large estate outside Rio de Janeiro and was a member of the Nelson Shipping Company, the owners of a fleet of refrigerated ships.

In 1935 Raymond Quilter had the good fortune to marry Margery Cooke, daughter of Sir Douglas Cooke, a well-known surgeon and Member of Parliament for Hammersmith. (He had fallen in love with her when she was a young girl and had to wait until she was considered old enough to be married. Meanwhile she had shared his enthusiasm for flying and they had spent many happy hours together at Brooklands.) She immediately gave Raymond the private support and encouragement he needed in the frustrating years ahead until GQ parachutes were officially accepted by the Air Ministry for use by the Royal Air Force. The Quilters went to live in Sussex near the Deans, and Gerald Dean became the godfather of their son.

Another two years passed in this fashion. The company did a small business in supplying parachute-carrying bags, windsocks and flare parachutes, and worked on the development of a combined parachute and flying suit which they called the Parasuit. The flexible packed parachute was only 1½ in thick and the whole suit weighed 23lb, including a silk lifebuoy which could be inflated by mouth or Sparklet. (A licence to manufacture the Parasuit in the United States was later sold to the Eagle Parachute Company.) They also made the Harnasuit, which incorporated a self-adjusting parachute harness with snap hooks for quick attachment to a breast-type parachute. This, too, included a lifebuoy, and both suits had quick releases for detaching the parachute on landing. Dagnall helped them to keep their part of the factory busy by giving them sub-contracts to make drogue targets for air-to-air gunnery practice and inflatable wind-direction indicators. A loss of £237 for the year to 31 March 1935 was turned into a profit of £246 in 1936.

At the board meeting in September that year Dagnall broke the news that owing to the flotation of RFD as a public company he could no longer continue as a director. In December his resignation was accepted and Dickinson was instructed to send him a letter thanking him for his past services to the company. At the same meeting Raymond Quilter reported that a new works he had found at Woking would be ready for occupation in the New Year.

For the next twenty-seven years the two companies were to go their separate ways, while always maintaining strong and friendly relations. The story of GQ Parachute's development in that period, and how in 1963 it was acquired by its 'parent', will be told in a later chapter.

CHAPTER FOUR

GOING PUBLIC

In 1936, encouraged by the faint-heartedness of Britain and France in the face of his treaty-breaking and aggression since he came to power three years earlier, Hitler seized and fortified the Rhineland and at the same time inaugurated a Four-Year Plan to make the German economy more self-sufficient in the event of war.

At home Winston Churchill, having failed to get a debate in secret session on the relative states of British and German armament, organised a deputation of Privy Councillors and others to Mr Baldwin, the Prime Minister, to lay before him the facts as they knew them. They were joined by a similar deputation from the House of Lords. Their representations were considered by the Ministers present and in November they were called together again by Mr Baldwin to receive a full statement. After pointing out that great efforts were being made to recover lost ground, Sir Thomas Inskip, the Government spokesman, said that no case existed which would justify the Government in adopting emergency measures.

Nevertheless, a few months earlier the Government had quietly taken steps to protect cities and installations against air attacks by ordering large numbers of barrage balloons. RFD were one of the two companies chosen as suppliers and in order to meet their output quota Dagnall had to raise fresh capital to provide increased manufacturing capacity.

This time he had to go beyond the local people who had provided the extra finances he had needed in 1934, so he decided to turn RFD into a public company. This was incorporated as the RFD Company Limited on 31 August 1936, the vending company being given as RFD Company (Holdings) Limited (formerly the RFD Company Limited). The authorised capital was increased to £75,000 made up of 750,000 shares of two shillings each, and a prospectus was drawn up in which the Ridgeford Trust, of 50 Pall Mall, London, offered 417,000 shares for sale at three shillings per share. When the list of subscriptions was opened on 14 September 1936, it was heavily over-subscribed at once.

RFD were described as manufacturers of flotation gear, pneumatic dinghies, balloons, flag targets, aerodrome wind indicators and other aeronautical equipment carrying on business at Guildford. The value attributed to the business was £38,000, made up as to:

	£	s	d
Goodwill	16,600	6	11
Patents, designs and patterns	8,000	0	0
Freehold property, plant, machinery etc.	7,289	0	0
Stocks, stores and work in progress	2,595	2	4
Sundry debtors	5,707	5	9
Cash in hand and at bank	170	11	11
	£40,362	6	11
Less creditors and income tax reserve	2,362	6	11
	£38,000	0	0

The purchase consideration payable to RFD Company (Holdings)— in which Dagnall had £4,100 of the £5,000 capital—was £26,500, made up of £19,000 in cash and the balance of £7,500 fully paid up two-shilling shares, while Dagnall personally received £11,500 by the allotment of 115,000 fully paid up shares.

After deducting the £19,000 cash consideration from the £31,000 obtained by the sale of the remaining shares at par, the sum of £12,000 was available for working capital, which the accountants, Andw W. Barr & Co, considered to be sufficient for the purposes of the company and for the extension of the works to meet the substantial increase in the contracts in hand.

The present writer has been unable to trace any records or accounts kept by Dagnall from the time he started the business in 1920 to the date of the incorporation of the company in 1936. It is of considerable interest, therefore, to read in the prospectus that the accountants reported the net profit for the three previous years as being:

For the year ended 31 December	1933	£2,251
,, ,, ,,	1934	£3,531
,, ,, ,,	1935	£5,096

The sales figures on which these modest profits were made are not shown.

As to the future, the prospectus stated that the company had in hand contracts to the value of more than £120,000. The barrage balloon contract was not mentioned specifically but presumably accounted for a large proportion of the order book. Dagnall expected to make a net profit of at least £10,000 in 1937. In the event, the net profit for the 15 months to the end of 1937 turned out to be £14,756.

The chairman of the Ridgeford Trust, Arthur Johnson OBE, was invited to become chairman of the new RFD Company but he declined and persuaded Edward Shrapnell-Smith CBE to accept the appointment. Shrapnell-Smith was not in the aviation world; he was a pioneer of commercial road transport, having organised the Lancashire Heavy Motor Trials in 1898/1900/1901. He later served on numerous Government road transport and petrol committees, and was now a director of the Aldershot and District Traction Co Ltd. Johnson wanted Anton van Beugen Bik, one of his colleagues in the Ridgeford Trust, to go on the RFD board, but Bik said he had too much on his plate already. Johnson then offered the directorship to Norman Hulbert, MP for Stockport and chairman of British Steel Construction (Birmingham) Ltd, who readily accepted. Dagnall was appointed managing director and a few months later Johnson himself was co-opted to the board.

As Anton Bik is going to play an important part in this history, it is appropriate to sketch in his background at this point. A Dutchman born in Sumatra, he had come to England from Holland as a young man in 1916 to work in the newly opened Mincing Lane office of his uncle's firm of rubber brokers in Amsterdam. He stayed there till 1923, when he married the daughter of the head of McLean Watson, the sugar brokers, who suggested that he might like to move into sugar. After a short time at the offices of Czarkinows, the international sugar company, he was sent on a two-year assignment to open a new office in Trieste. On his return he went back to his first love, rubber, working on his own account as a dealer. In the course of a rather tricky negotiation with the Sorbo Company at Woking, he asked to see one of the directors, who turned out to be Arthur Johnson. At that time Johnson was working for Philip Hill, but he was about to start his own investment trust and was looking for partners. Impressed with Bik's handling of the Sorbo affair, Johnson asked him to become a director of the Ridgeford Trust.

How it all started: the first RFD product made at Hersham, Surrey, in 1920. Emergency flotation bags for a Short Brothers aircraft, shown ready for dispatch and installed inside the fuselage. The company also undertook to supply 'every description of Rope, Wire and Fabric Work, Balloons, etc., etc'

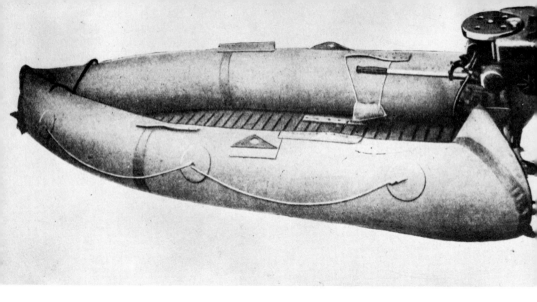

(*above*) The 1929 version of the RFD inflatable was a pleasure boat costing £16 complete with a pair of sculls. A transom was provided for fitting an outboard motor. It was packed in a valise weighing 55lb and could be inflated in three minutes by the exhaust of a car or motor-cycle; (*below*) Dagnall's pencilled comment on the back of this photograph of himself and C. Howarth of the Air Ministry during trials of the automatic inflation head was 'if we, RFD, don't watch it, the ruddy dinghy will capsize.' The valise in which the dinghy was packed can be seen in the water

Dagnall, it will be noticed, was the only executive director; nobody else in the old company was—or was suitable to be—appointed to the new board. But this did not mean, as he quickly found out, that he could go on running the show single-handed, with one or two trusted subordinates, as he had done since the begining. The formation of the public company was a turning-point not only for RFD but for Dagnall himself. His friends had to remind him that he no longer owned the business; he had sold it, and it was now owned by the shareholders. As managing director he had to account to the board of directors, who were strangers. Reg Dagnall found this hard to accept; he had acted individually for so long that he could not readily change the habits and outlook of a lifetime. For the rest of his life he was never really happy in the company.

But this did not prevent him being the same kindly man who looked after his workpeople and earned their loyalty. As the boss of a small business he had the invaluable advantage of being able to call them by their first names and to take off his coat and show a new operator how the job should be done. Small parties of them were invited to have a day's outing on the boat he now kept at Lee-on-Solent, where he had bought a seaside house.

In the same month of 1936 that the RFD Company was incorporated, Dagnall formed a £100 company called Dagnall Aircraft Limited, for the purpose of carrying on the business of engineers, founders, smiths, aeronautical experts, consultants, etc, but he made it clear that there was no intention of operating the company for the time being.

As there was no room to expand at Guildford, a new works-cum-inflation shed was erected and equipped at Catteshall Lane, Godalming, at a cost of £14,000 and soon became a local landmark known as 'the balloon factory'. When it was ready for occupation early in 1937 Percy Williams was put in charge, later being appointed general manager. Williams had joined Dagnall in 1928 as a draughtsman at Guildford and eventually became works manager. He made a useful contribution to the development of the RFD glider, and from 1934 onwards he had been responsible for a considerable share of the company's design work on dinghies. He brought experience and talent to the work, which yielded good results whenever he could subdue his peculiar temperament.

The early barrage balloons were of the LZ (low zone) type, and for the first few years—until the outbreak of war—complete balloons were produced at Godalming.

As the threat of war increased in 1939 an underground air-raid shelter, complete with ventilation system, was built in the front garden of Dagnall's house in Farnham Road, Guildford, on the Air Ministry's instructions—an indication of the value placed on his safety.

CHAPTER FIVE

'DINGHY, DINGHY!'

When war was declared in September 1939 it was realised that the requirements for barrage balloons had been underestimated, and that the combined production capacity of Dunlop and RFD was insufficient. In 1940 the Ministry put the whole RFD operation on a broader footing. P. B. Cow were given the job of making the front sections of the balloons and J. Mandelberg & Company were made responsible for the rear sections. RFD put the two together and assembled the complete balloon. Mandelbergs also proofed the fabric, which was mostly supplied—as might be expected—by Perseverance Mill.

By 1940 there were between 600 and 700 girls working on balloons at Godalming and everyone thought that production could not be improved until one day Lord Beaverbrook, who had been put in charge of the Ministry of Aircraft Production by Winston Churchill to speed up the output of the aviation industry, suddenly appeared at Catteshall Lane. He was amazed and shocked to find the factory working a single shift. 'You must start a night shift immediately,' he commanded.

Realising that they would be asked the next day what they had done about it, and with little spare labour in the district to draw on, the management sent home some of the girls to have a rest so that they could report back later to start a night shift that very night! Then they set about scouring the neighbourhood for extra girls.

In 1940 a different type of barrage balloon was made, the change being probably due to the need to save rubber. The LZ-C balloon differed in aspect ratio and in fineness ratio, and was slightly larger in volume (19,500cu ft). Then, when the sea war became intense, RFD moved over to the convoy type of balloon, which was much smaller (5,000 to 6,000cu ft). Minor changes were continually made to the convoy balloon and when the war ended it had been developed to the Mark 13 model.

Barrage balloons were also manufactured by a number of firms totally lacking in previous experience. Some of these firms were brought in as sub-contractors at RFD's instigation and the company freely helped them by training their staff and advising on technical and production problems. As a sideline RFD carried out the initial development work on a scheme by which large numbers of free balloons with bombs attached could be released in the anticipated path of enemy bombers. This method of defence was tried out on a restricted scale with balloons supplied by other contractors.

As the war slowly got under way the demand for inflatable dinghies increased to such an extent that by 1940 a score of other companies had to be brought in to meet the expanded aircraft programme. All the circular dinghies produced by these firms were made to RFD designs. They included two small circular dinghies known as the L and M types with accommodation for two and three men respectively which were taken up by the Ministry and subsequently produced in large quantities —but not by RFD, who made only the prototypes. The contracts all went to the newcomers, partly because many of them had only restricted space for manufacture. Production of these small dinghies suited them very well and they made certain of filling their available production capacity by quoting prices which were sometimes uneconomic. If deficiencies occurred they were financed from their normal trading activities, which ranged from football pools to corsets and stockings. After the war all but three of these miscellaneous firms that had been given wartime contracts to make dinghies dropped out of the business entirely when their contracts were cancelled. The three that carried on—Greengate & Irwell Rubber Company, Elliott Equipment (a subsidiary of P. B. Cow) and Lea Bridge Rubber Works —continued to furnish the Ministry of Supply with quotations for dinghies based on original design work done by RFD.

Meanwhile it had been found that inflatable dinghies stowed loose in a blow-out compartment or inside the aircraft were liable to get so knocked about that their reliability and efficiency were seriously reduced. Accordingly in 1938 the RFD Company, at the request of the Air Ministry, designed a valise-type container in which the dinghy and signalling equipment were packed. This consisted of an outer valise laced with cordage of a strength that would break when the dinghy inflated and exerted sufficient pressure on the cord, leaving the dinghy free to inflate fully; an inner container attached to the dinghy housed the signalling equipment and was recovered by the occupants of the dinghy after they had got on board.

Except on aircraft with dinghies carried in blow-out panels, the valise—containing the dinghy, inflation head, carbon dioxide bottle and separate signalling equipment container—was located inside the fuselage near the exit door. It was held in position by a quick-release 'safety belt' so that the package could not foul aircraft controls passing through the fuselage and would not injure the crew by becoming a projectile on the impact of ditching. The RAF worked out a highly efficient ditching drill culminating in the urgent cry 'dinghy, dinghy!' As soon as the aircraft came to rest on the water the valise was detached and a cord from it was fastened to a strong point on the aircraft. The valise was then thrown out of the exit door by one member of the crew. The cord was connected to the cable operating the cam on the Dagnall G-type head and the pull as the valise was thrown out caused the head to release the carbon dioxide and inflate the dinghy, which thereupon burst out of the valise and was ready for occupation—the cord serving as a painter. In operational use the equipment had the great merit of speed and simplicity. The dinghy was launched in its most compact form and the ancillary equipment required by the survivors, having been launched by the same physical movement, was immediately to hand.

The equipment containers were originally designed to hold two marine distress signals and a pump for topping up the dinghy. These were sufficient before the war, but long operational flights and delay in picking up survivors owing to bad weather or enemy action necessitated many additions. These were worked out by the Department RDS3 of the Air Ministry (which became the Ministry of Aircraft Production) where the work on research and development in connection with dinghies carried on by C. Howarth before the war was now in the charge of Basil Townsend, with whom Dagnall formed a close relationship. Townsend's ideas were put into effect in 1941 when RFD in conjunction with other contractors produced a number of compartmented boxes varying in size according to the number of the crew, to go inside the equipment container. These emergency packs covered four separate functions:

Further equipment required in connection with the dinghy— bellows, baler, paddles, and weather cover to protect the crew.

Signalling equipment—marine distress signals, Very pistol, helio-graph, radio or radar set, and means for elevating the aerial (balloon or kite).

Survival equipment—tinned water or chemical means for making sea water drinkable, self-heating soup, fruit juice, concentrated food, and fishing net.

Sundries—first-aid outfit, maps, instruction books, playing cards, etc.

Only one of the three emergency packs was made in quantity by RFD, 18,500 of them being supplied to the RAF between November 1941 and the end of the war.

It was sometimes necessary to drop equipment to survivors swimming around in the water. In these cases aircraft such as Lysanders, Defiants, Thunderbolts and Spitfires dropped valises containing dinghies and emergency packs as near to them as they could. The dinghy was inflated by the Dagnall head during its descent as a result of the pull on the cam-operating cable when the valise left the aircraft.

So far all the dinghies made by RFD had been of the circular type, whereas American and German inflatable dinghies were boat-shaped. Boat-shaped dinghies were admittedly better suited for propulsion, but the circular dinghy retained a greater degree of rigidity because forces applied to the floor did not distort the buoyancy chamber to any extent. The circular buoyancy chamber (inflated to less than 2 psi) was also less affected by the inevitable leakage that took place in all inflatables, and the circular dinghy was more economical in terms of weight and volume of stowage for a given buoyancy requirement. Finally, it was argued that the circular dinghy, being unable to move far from the aircraft, which radioed its position when it ditched, was more easily located by rescue craft. The boat-shaped or oval raft was at a disadvantage in this respect, tending to lie broadside to the wind and waves, which caused it to drift.

Nevertheless two boat-shaped dinghies were produced by RFD and other contractors for special purposes. The first was the K-type single-seater dinghy for fighter pilots forced down in the sea. During the Battle of Britain and for some time afterwards the RAF fighter pilot who baled out over the sea had to depend for survival on his Mae West life-jacket (many of which were made by RFD), whereas the Luftwaffe pilot had the comparative luxury of a one-man dinghy. A specimen fell into British hands when a German pilot was picked up by air–sea rescue launch. It was sent down to Godalming, where Williams evaluated it and produced the prototype of an equivalent version. This was taken over by Townsend at the Ministry of Aircraft Production, who gave it to P. B. Cow for detailed development (P. B. Cow acted as the Ministry's design and drawing office). At first it was manufactured as an open dinghy carried in a compartment of the pilot's parachute pack (which he sat on); then it was given a single-skin canopy to provide some protection from the wind and water; and finally it was equipped with a mast and sail to help the pilot get away from an enemy shore. RFD shared in the development of the canopy with P. B. Cow and made a small number of dinghies towards the end of the war, but they did not participate in the main contracts for the 350,000 K-type dinghies manufactured during the war as their capacity was already fully occupied.

The second boat-shaped dinghy was produced in 1942 in response to an invitation by the Ministry of Aircraft Production to design and supply a dinghy for a particular purpose in competition with Dunlop and P. B. Cow. The requirement was for an inflatable with good sailing qualities to accommodate up to eight men. A dinghy of this kind was needed for the crews of large bombers in case they had to ditch near the enemy-occupied coast on returning from raids over Europe. Rescue aircraft or launches sent out to the assistance of such crews in circular dinghies were themselves being attacked and frequently disabled, which multiplied the task of follow-up rescue parties. A good sailing dinghy would enable many crews to reach safety unaided. The RFD design was accepted and the Q-type sailing dinghy went into production in 1943. RFD were responsible for 5,000 of the 10,000 hulls made during the war. The masts, sails, rudders, etc, were supplied by other contractors, and close liaison was maintained with them through Robert Bicknell, a RAF officer with pre-war boating experience who had already worked with RFD on an oval-shaped sailing inflatable dinghy which was the forerunner of the Q- and S-type sailing dinghies. Some later development work on the Q-type dinghy was done by P. B. Cow's central design and drawing office for the Government. The S-type sailing dinghy was developed at the Cardington research centre run by J. W. W. Dyer, who later joined RFD to set up the company's laboratory.

The RFD Company obtained letters patent in respect of the keel (jointly with Percy Williams) and rudder (jointly with A. van Beugen

59

Bik) of the Q-type dinghy but no claim was made in respect of these inventions as the company was remunerated to the extent of £765 for the development work done on the dinghy, though there were no clauses in the development contracts obliging them to pass on the benefit of the inventions to the Government without further payment.

The boat-shaped sailing dinghy was the basis of the seaplane tender which was used by Catalinas and other flying boats for ferrying stores from the shore. The first tenders supplied by RFD had oars, but later they were equipped with an outboard motor so that they could reach the coast in the event of a forced landing. Once again the avoidance of any damage to the flying boat's hull when the dinghy bumped along-side was a strong point in the inflatable's favour.

From the RFD point of view, the major technical success of the war was the Dagnall head for inflating dinghies with carbon dioxide. The idea of using an electric current to explode a cartridge to release the liquid gas from the cylinder (instead of the hydrostatic valves and pneumatic head employed in the Walter Kidde system) was certainly brilliant. No special source of current was needed, because batteries were commonly installed in aircraft, and there was no other require-ment for electric current when the aircraft ditched. The cartridge as a means of providing the power to operate the cutter was ideal because the explosion gave lots of power quickly. Dagnall, who was really a specialist in rubberised textiles, beat at their own game some of the foremost carbon dioxide engineers in the world, as was shown when Walter Kidde recognised the merit of the Dagnall head and took out manufacturing licences under his patents.

Except for the K-type single-seat dinghy and some dinghies with a manually operated head carried by seaplanes, all inflatable dinghies used in the war by the British Services incorporated inflation heads based on Dagnall designs.

The heads were also used on two other types of air–sea rescue equipment. The first was the airborne lifeboat, which was a clinker-built wooden dinghy with an outboard motor dropped by parachutes from Lancaster, Warwick and Hudson aircraft to crews afloat in inflatable dinghies with long distances to traverse. The Ministry en-trusted the development of the idea to Uffa Fox in the Isle of Wight, and Robert Bicknell was sent down to help him. Bicknell turned to RFD for the design and construction of self-righting buoyancy chambers fitted fore and aft which would inflate automatically and

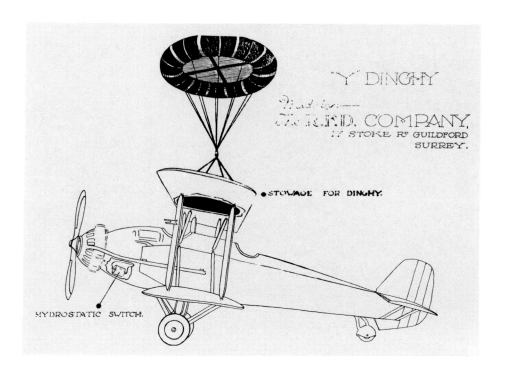

'Y' DINGHY

...R.F.D. COMPANY,
17 STOKE Rᵈ GUILDFORD
SURREY.

• STOWAGE FOR DINGHY.

HYDROSTATIC SWITCH.

The pictures tell the story. When an aircraft ditched, the Youngman dinghy made by RFD was released from a compartment in the centre of the main plane and kept the aircraft afloat. The original idea was to use a balloon, but this was abandoned in favour of a lifebelt, which Robert Youngman converted into a dinghy by adding a floor. The action photograph was taken during trials held in 1933 in conjunction with HMS *Ark Royal*

Dagnall's experience of making observation balloons for Airships Limited during World War I was called upon to make barrage balloons in a new factory at Godalming when the threat of war returned in the mid-1930s. RFD turned out 100 a month throughout World War II. The lower picture shows LZC-type balloons with women handling-crews at Cardington

The first informal meeting of the London Gliding Club was organised by Reginald Dagnall at Stoke Park Farm, Guildford, in March 1930, when his 'Dagling' glider was pitted against the original German Zögling

The Perseverance Mill Company, which joined RFD in 1959, supplied the fabric for most of the British and American rigid airships built between the wars, including the ill-fated R.101 seen here moored at Cardington in 1929

prevent the boat overturning when it splashed down. RFD delivered the goods and the lifeboat went into service, but it was later abandoned because of the special modifications that had to be made to aircraft in order to stow it—and above all because only one lifeboat could be carried.

These objections did not apply to the second device, called the Lindholme gear, which provided extra supplies for aircrews in dinghies likely to take some time to rescue. (The primary equipment in the aircraft dinghy was strictly limited.) The gear took the form of a series of cylindrical cardboard containers (usually five) in which were packed an extra dinghy, dry clothing, food, signalling equipment and other items. These containers were dropped from the bomb bay of an aircraft in the same way as a stick of bombs. Joined to one another by floating cord, the containers were dropped to leeward of the crew in the dinghy, which then drifted into the floating cord. On striking the water the extra dinghy was automatically inflated and burst out of the container. It then sustained the remaining containers until the crew could reach them. The same system was developed to help single survivors.

Lindholme gear was so called because it was developed by Squadron Leader Huxford, an engineer officer stationed at RAF Lindholme on the low-lying Hatfield Moors in Yorkshire in 1940–41. As reported in the *Daily Telegraph* (30 January 1979), this airfield was the scene of the extraordinary fate that befell a Wellington bomber with a Polish crew which struggled home in a crippled state from a mission over the Continent only to crash in Lindholme Bog, 500 yards short of the runway, and sink beneath the swamp without trace. This gave rise to stories of a ghostly mud-stained figure that appeared in the district at night enquiring the way to station sick quarters or the operations room. The airfield was not used for twenty-five years after the war, but the wreckage of the Wellington came to light when the bog was drained in the early 1970s. The remains of the unidentified crew were buried in the local churchyard and the ghost was seen no more.

As the pioneers of the H- and J-type dinghies, which were extensively used by the Royal Air Force, RFD could justly claim to have been responsible for many thousands of the 17,000 members of Allied aircrews saved by liferafts after ditching during the war. The numbers saved might have been greater if the value of inflatable canopies as protection had been realised earlier, since many airmen who had successfully survived ditching were dead from exposure when they were lifted from their dinghies.

In addition to saving lives, inflatable dinghies had a very important psychological effect on aircrews. When they went out on a sortie they knew that if they had to use their dinghy equipment they could rely upon it absolutely; and if they had to take to their dinghies the whole force of the Air–Sea Rescue would be directed towards locating and saving them. There must have been cases, too, where a pilot returning from a sortie over the Continent with a badly damaged aircraft hesitated subconsciously when he came to the sea crossing with the doubt in his mind as to whether or not his aircraft would make it. The knowledge that his emergency equipment was not wanting in any respect would fortify his natural desire to go on. Aircraft successfully brought back in these circumstances represented a double saving in the machine and in the continued availability of skilled aircrew, who might otherwise have fallen into enemy hands.

In 1941 Dagnall wrote to the Ministry of Aircraft Production requesting permission to start a 'Silverfish Club' for airmen who owed their lives to a rubber dinghy on the lines of the Caterpillar Club for airmen who had been saved by their parachutes and the Late Arrivals Club for those who had walked home through the enemy lines. Instead of welcoming this morale-raising suggestion the men at the Ministry frowned on it, hinting at possible security considerations. Nothing more was heard of the idea until after Dagnall's death, when it was revived in a letter to *The Aeroplane* by someone signing himself 'Just a Lobster'—his suggestion being a 'Lobster Club' for those who had been lobbed into the sea and had some 'dinghy hours'. P. B. Cow then put up a scheme for a 'Goldfish Club', and this time the Ministry gave their consent. A badge showing a small goldfish with a wing attached was embroidered on a piece of black cloth and was worn under the airman's jacket lapel. A blue silk bar was added for more than one rescue.

Besides manufacturing barrage balloons and dinghies in great quantities, RFD also worked on a number of other products during the war, most of which were of only passing value to the company. But they included one that was to lay the foundations of a future RFD subsidiary company.

It began early in 1940 when a visitor arrived at the 'drawing office' at Guildford run by the works manager, Charles Fellowes, and his young assistant Fred Scott. He announced himself as Lieutenant L.

Stanley Bell from the Admiralty, and he explained that he had been given the job of resuscitating the gunnery training device which had been used on the deck of HMS *President* on the Thames in the First World War. The device consisted of a plaster dome inside which gunners under training aimed a light anti-aircraft gun at moving pictures of aeroplanes thrown on the 'sky' from a 35mm cine-projector. An up-to-date version was urgently needed to speed up the initial training of naval gunners by means of a portable device which would save the time spent in driving to ranges and wasting live ammunition. It could also be used in the docks to train seamen in the use of the anti-aircraft guns now being supplied to merchant ships.

Bell wanted to supply a portable dome comprising a canopy of balloon fabric stretched over a light framework made of 1in metal conduit, but Fellowes had a much simpler idea: why not make the device in one piece, including the floor, by inflating a complete fabric structure? This would meet the requirement of quick and easy portability more satisfactorily. The whole thing could be packed up on a 3-ton lorry and driven from station to station.

The RFD suggestion was accepted and the dome for the gunnery trainer went into production at Godalming. It had a diameter of 20ft and was made of 2-ply balloon fabric. RFD made only the dome; the internal equipment was developed by Bell in a little place at Cranleigh provided for him by the Admiralty and was made in Admiralty workshops.

The gunner in the dome trainer did everything but fire—the seat, the sight and the controls were those of an actual gun, but there was no barrel. The sound of the gun was accurately reproduced, varying with the rate of firing, and a sound-track was added to the film to simulate the noises of a real dive-bombing attack. Films depicting various target profiles were held in a 'library'. The selected film was fed into a 35mm projector which threw it on to a mirror, which in turn deflected it on to the dome. The mirror exactly reproduced the swinging movements of the camera when the original 'attack' was photographed. This was effected by recording the movements on a cam, which was synchronised with the film and actuated the mirror.

At first the domes were equipped with the mountings and sights of Oerlikons, double Brownings, and Marlins supplied by the United States under lease-lend. Later, some Bofors guns were also used. Production continued throughout the war, but never on a very large scale.

Bell's own account of the early development of the Portabel, as the device came to be called, is contained in the claim he filed with the Royal Commission of Awards to Inventors after the war (it is believed he was paid £20,000). The claim, together with the correspondence, is kept at the Public Records Office at Kew, but will remain tantalisingly secret until 1982 under the thirty-year rule. (The post-war development of the Portabel, and the present-day simulators derived from it and made by RFD Systems Engineering, are described in Chapter Twelve).

For many years before the war RFD had been the principal suppliers of sleeve and flag targets towed behind aircraft for air-to-air and ground-to-air gunnery practice. To meet the advanced techniques required for actual warfare, the company co-operated with the Government departments and Services in designing and producing targets that could be towed at much higher speeds and others that would give a response to radar signals.

When Hitler unleashed eighty-nine divisions of the German Army on the Lowlands on 10 May 1940 in *Operation Yellow* as a prelude to over-running Northern France, one of the few counter-initiatives the Allies were able to take was *Operation Royal Marine*, a project for immobilising barge traffic on the Rhine and thereby disrupting the German Army's line of communication. The idea had been conceived by Winston Churchill himself and consisted of floating large quantities of fluvial mines in the river from French territory above Strasbourg. They would be carried down by the current and hopefully create havoc by damaging any barges or pontoon bridges that happened to lie in their path. The mines (called W-bombs) were quite small—not much bigger than a football—and carried 20lb of explosives. They were developed by a small War Office (later Ministry of Defence) unit specialising in secret weapons, which had started work in the previous November. During testing on Walton reservoir it was found that they benefited by being fitted with fabric drogues, and RFD were called in to supply them. A rigid timetable was set for completion of the contract, and it was only met by casting everything else aside in the Guildford factory for the time being. In the first week after the German advance began, 1,700 mines were floated and produced immediate results. Nearly all the traffic on the section of the Rhine between Karlsruhe and Mainz was paralysed, and the Karlsruhe barrage and several pontoon bridges were badly damaged. Unhappily, as Churchill remarked in *The Second World War*, 'the success of the device was lost in the deluge of disaster'.

The initial order was for 10,000 W-bombs, but twice that number were eventually produced, some being dropped in rivers and canals by low-flying aircraft.

After the evacuation from Dunkirk, large numbers of kapok life-jackets issued to the troops were collected at the points of disembarkation and many were sent to RFD to be overhauled and renovated. The majority were in a dreadful state after long immersion in the water and being roughly handled. Godalming and Guildford were full up, so the work was done at temporary premises the company were asked to occupy at Brighton. There was a wide choice of premises available, for with the enemy only a few miles away on the French coast, Brighton had lost most of its trade. At first it was suggested that RFD should take over the buildings on the Palace Pier—if not the Aquarium—but they settled for a large building previously shared by Woolworths and a firm of chemists in the town, plus the Dubarry cosmetics factory at Hove. Mrs Dobson was sent down to recruit a workforce from the local women and girls, who were quite unfamiliar with this kind of work—indeed, they took 80 minutes to do a job that the skilled Godalming staff could do in a quarter of the time.

Later in 1940, when the Government decided to use gliders for airborne landings, the company handed over the whole of its drawings and technical data of RFD gliders and sailplanes to the General Aircraft Company without fee, recompense or acknowledgement of any kind.

By 1941 the Ministry of Aircraft Production were faced with the increasing problem of salvaging large numbers of bombers that were damaged—but not beyond repair—when they crash-landed on returning to base from missions over the Continent. They designed a lifting gear made of inflatable bags so that the aircraft could be retrieved without further damage and asked RFD among others to tender for its manufacture. Reginald Dagnall virtually cut himself out of the running by refusing to submit his working drawings to the Ministry—he could be very stiff-necked on occasion, and by now his health was beginning to fail—so the contract went to Dunlop, Siebe Gorman and Philips. But RFD were to benefit later from the lessons learnt in this initial work on lifting gear, as we shall see.

In the preparations for the invasion of Normandy RFD took a prominent part in the design and production of full-scale dummy tanks, guns and trucks made of rubberised materials that were used to deceive enemy air reconnaissance by simulating large concentrations of vehicles.

The early specimens were crudely made up of inflatable bags, a framework of metal rods, and balloon fabric draped over the whole structure. With their distorted flat surfaces and ill-defined shadows, they were barely accurate enough to qualify for their official description of 'low-fidelity decoys'. Towards the end of the war RFD found the answer in a new kind of fabric consisting of two layers of cloth linked together by a series of tie-threads which also held them apart. This slab material, as it was called, produced inflatable dummy vehicles with flat surfaces and a much sharper, more clearly defined silhouette that effectively deceived enemy reconnaissance aircrews when they were used with the Allied armies advancing towards Germany. Indeed they proved to be of such sound construction that two dummy amphibious DUKWS were actually used for ferrying $1\frac{1}{2}$-ton loads of stores across the Rhine.

The complete tally of RFD production during the war does not seem to have been recorded, but in his chairman's speech at the annual general meeting at the end of 1944 (five months before V-E Day) Edward Shrapnell-Smith reported that since the beginning of the war in 1939 the company had produced nearly 29,000 balloons of various kinds, 41,000 dinghies and inflatable boats, flotation gear for 11,000 aircraft, 1,000 sets of flotation gear for airborne lifeboats, and over 100,000 towed targets for aircraft and anti-aircraft practice, as well as a large variety of accessories and spare parts far too numerous to mention.

Unhappily Reginald Dagnall did not live to see the full value of his products to the British war effort. In the autumn of 1941 his health, undermined by a combination of bronchial weakness and heavy smoking, deteriorated to the point when he had to give up visiting the factories at Guildford and Godalming and in the last nine months of his life no one in the company saw him. He died of cancer, greatly lamented by his colleagues and workpeople, on 16 November 1942. He was fifty-four.

Dagnall was succeeded as managing director by Anton van Beugen Bik, who had finally yielded to the pressure of Arthur Johnson and had joined the board as a non-executive director in May 1939. It was hoped that he would get Dagnall and Williams to work together in spite of their mutual dislike, which might easily have torn the company apart. From all accounts the unfortunate Williams, who suffered from asthma, was difficult to work with or for at the best of times, yet no one could deny his brilliance as a designer. On top of this personal antipathy, there were all the elements of discord in their respective positions: Dagnall the managing director at the Guildford headquarters, with its small factory, and Williams in charge of the new and much larger branch factory at Godalming. And though Williams had been appointed technical director by the board, Dagnall had his own determined ideas on technical matters. Altogether, Bik had his hands full. It meant that he had to spend more time at the factories than he would normally have done as a non-executive director, and in the event this was just as well, for it gave him a valuable insight into the operation of a manufacturing business which he had not previously experienced.

Six months before Dagnall's death Bik was made an executive director, following about a year in responsible charge of large sections of the business under Dagnall's direction. During that time he got great satisfaction from dealing with the staff, who quickly came to like and admire him. He could hardly keep away from the place and would spend week-ends shifting the work tables around to improve the production flow, so that the staff never quite knew what to expect on Monday mornings. They nick-named him 'Mr Carter Patterson'.

CHAPTER SIX

ANYTHING GOES

The end of the Second World War was also very nearly the end of RFD. All Government contracts, which meant *all* contracts—for the company had no other customer—were abruptly cancelled. The danger had of course been foreseen and various products that would supplement any business on offer from Government departments and the aviation industry after the war had been examined as soon as ultimate victory was in sight, but only one had got beyond the investigation stage.

Indeed, after V-J Day in September 1945 the immediate future looked so bleak that there were times when Anton Bik was inclined to think it might be wiser to close down the company straight away than to struggle on until such time as sufficient new business could be found to fully occupy the works (the Godalming factory now had an area of 120,000sq ft, six times larger than in 1936) and to employ the workforce, which was nearly 1,000 strong. It was the plight of the workforce—not so much the wartime workers as the hard core of long-service people—that finally decided him to soldier on. He courageously told them that no one would be sacked, while at the same time recommending as many as possible to look for jobs elsewhere. Most of them sensibly realised that the company could not go on paying them when there was so little work to do. They took Bik at his word, and after a few months the payroll dwindled to about 250.

In the post-war years up to the end of the 1950s (when amalgamation with its traditional textile suppliers changed it from an individual company to the nucleus of a group), RFD developed a range of avaiation and marine liferafts that became the mainstay of the business. At the same time various other projects were put in hand. To attempt to describe all the company's activities in this period chronologically would disrupt the main narrative. It is therefore proposed to deal with the secondary projects first and to reserve the story of the company's most important product for the next chapter.

(*right*) Anton van Beugen Bik who carried on the RFD Company after Dagnall's death and masterminded its growth into the present RFD Group

(*below*) Reginald Foster Dagnall (1888–1942), founder of the RFD Company. A portrait taken in his Guildford office shortly before he died

James Gregory (1902–1962), (*above*) and Sir Reginald Quilter (1902–1959), the founders of the GQ Parachute Company, which became part of the RFD Group in 1964

To start with, any job was welcome, and various things from beach balls to shopping bags and inflatable chairs were turned out at Godalming to keep the wolf from the door. There was plenty of material in the stocks of Government-owned fabric stored underneath the factory —orange and silver fabric had been positioned strategically in various parts of the country by the Government, which controlled all supplies during the war. On the other hand the Guildford factory went over entirely to making up garments from materials supplied by the clothing manufacturers, notably women's jackets and skirts for Jantzen (better known for their swim suits) and little girls' dresses and pinafores for Fairy Fox, a short-lived subsidiary formed by RFD. But the garment-making business was not a success and it folded up in 1948 for lack of orders. The Guildford factory—the scene of Dagnall's early efforts in building up the RFD Company—was sold.

Meanwhile the company had found an alternative market in the field of protective clothing made of specially treated fabrics. It had started immediately after the war when the Iranian Oil Company asked RFD to produce a range of chemical-proof clothing and headgear for refinery and pipe-line work in their Middle East refineries, and in the following years a steady business was done in supplying these items to other oil companies, chemical plants and the iron and steel industry. In the late 1950s the RFD/Heinke breathing apparatus was approved for use on merchant ships.

Compared with the conventional kapok-filled life-saving jacket, an inflatable jacket was particularly attractive to airline operators on account of its light weight, which made up for the very slight risk of its being punctured. Immediately after the war ended in 1945 RFD started developing a new life-jacket for the civil airline market based on the wartime Cunliffe belt-type jacket, and by 1947 production was in full swing. The RFD Type PW45 jacket met with approval on all sides, and the first deliveries were made to de Havilland at Hatfield for the forthcoming Comet airliner—the first turbo-jet to go into commercial service.

Working in conjunction with Lieutenant Phillips of the Admiralty, the company then turned its attention to a similar jacket for marine use. By 1950 it had been adopted by the British, American and Canadian navies and was being evaluated by many other countries. The civil version, called the Type 51, was the lightest on the market and incorporated a number of new features including an improved water-activated lamp which was switched on automatically when the jacket was immersed.

RFD was able to make use of its earlier skills in supplying a 45,000cu ft spherical balloon for training parachutists at Cardington. This was followed by a contract to supply balloons for the same purpose in Belgium, and repeat orders from the British Government. The balloon used in the enterprise *Small World* was also made at Godalming.

The new project on which some preparatory work had been done during the war was textile printing. This process had been carried on by a company, Amersham Printers (in the Buckinghamshire town of that name), who were sub-contractors to RFD, making flotation bags for Swordfish and Wellington aircraft. They had a competent manager named J. Aitchison who approached Bik in 1944 with the suggestion that RFD should start a similar business under his direction. Bik, looking for new lines of business when peace returned, accepted Aitchison's proposal, and some preliminary planning and staff training were done while the war was still on.

The printing of textiles got under way slowly at Godalming in 1945 because of delays in the delivery and installation of the necessary equipment due to the Government deciding in their wisdom to allocate most new textile machinery to exports. The business was run as commission printers—printing on customers' own materials—and a team of designers was taken on to produce attractive patterns. Before long, differences of opinion about manufacturing policy began to appear, Aitchison wanting to supply the low-priced apparel field while Bik was all for concentrating on high quality piece goods for interior furnishing and dress materials, arguing that their capacity was too small to tackle the mass market. Bik had his way and good orders were received from such high-class firms as Liberty's and Sanderson's, but production did not get into full swing until towards the end of 1945 with the result that textile printing was wholly responsible for the trading loss of £32,010 sustained by the company in the year ended 31 December.

In 1949 the section was dignified with a name of its own, Weyvale Fabric Printworks, but it never fulfilled the hopes initially held for it. The fuel crisis of 1947 had caused stoppages which affected production for some time, and then sales had been hit by the increase in purchase tax to $66\frac{2}{3}$ per cent in 1948. On top of this came a restriction on imports in a number of valuable markets. By the early 1950s business was so poor that a major part of its floor space was released for the benefit of the aeronautical equipment division.

Textile printing came to an end as a result of a near-disaster that befell the company in 1954. On the night of 17 August fire broke out in the Godalming factory and quickly devastated about half of it before the Surrey Fire Brigade brought it under control. It was a spectacular fire, the raging flames being accompanied by the continual explosion of carbon dioxide cylinders. The cause was never discovered. The dinghy shops, the balloon shop, the stores and the secretarial, accounts and record offices were all destroyed, and only the front entrance, the engineering shop and the textile printing factory escaped unscathed.

Bik was called from his bed at 3 am and arrived at Catteshall Lane just in time to see his office go up in flames. The macabre thought crossed his mind that on his desk were the ashes of a colleague who had been cremated a few days earlier which he had undertaken to dispose of in accordance with his wishes. The double cremation, he reflected, had taken care of that.

When the workpeople arrived at 8.30 am Bik promised that no one would be stood off. Urgent calls were put through to the overseas companies to send back duplicate copies of all the technical records they had been supplied with when they were formed, to replace the originals destroyed in the fire. A major part of the stocks of materials used by the aeronautical division had been lost, and their replacement presented a serious problem. Meanwhile everyone set about clearing up the mess and work tables were set up in the undamaged areas of the factory. In fact only one complete day's work was lost and next morning the factory was operating again—although on a very reduced scale.

Bik appealed for volunteers to help the company's maintenance men rebuild the ruined shops and offices, for the quicker the factory was restored to full working order, the sooner they would be able to get back to their proper jobs. No outside building contractors were employed. The trade unions fully co-operated by suspending the customary demarcation rules in recognition of the concern the company had shown in maintaining full employment in times of crisis—in the first place immediately after the war, and now in the aftermath of the fire.

In re-allocating the workload in what was left of the factory while it was being rebuilt, priority was given to the dinghies and towed targets of the aeronautical division, which had a full order book and had lost its workshops in the fire. The company were only too glad to seize the opportunity to cut their losses and close down the Weyvale Fabric Printworks in order to release its floor space for more remunerative work. Only a small section engaged in dyeing and finishing textiles was retained. (It is only fair to add that the fabric printworks had its champions on the staff who believed that it was about to turn the corner when the fire hastened its closure. Given a little more time—it was argued—the operation would have become viable.)

Soon after the war an invitation came out of the blue from Sweden for RFD to demonstrate the Portabel gunnery trainer. A few spare domes were available in the factory, and Bik obtained the internal apparatus required to make up a complete trainer from Stanley Bell, who had retired from the Navy with the rank of Lieutenant-Commander and had bought up the components used in the Portabel from surplus Government stocks. Accompanied by Stanley Bell and his right-hand man, a competent technician named Bishop, Bik set off on what turned out to be a highly successful Scandinavian tour. Sweden, Norway and Finland all placed orders for trainers, and when he was in Norway Bik received a telegram from a Danish admiral inviting him to visit Denmark on his way home. While he was about it, he called in on the authorities in Holland and Belgium as well. He came home with a nicely filled order book.

On his return Bik acquired the manufacturing rights of the complete device from Bell, who was operating from a workshop at Rodborough, near Guildford, and was engrossed in plans to make a ball-point pen. This was followed up in 1953 by RFD acquiring Bell's small engineering company with its goodwill and designs—including the Portabel—for the sum of £3,751.

RFD were now responsible for supplying all the internal apparatus, including the electrical supply and circuits, as well as the dome. Bell's stock of apparatus, which the company acquired, was soon used up. A few of the major components then had to be obtained from outside suppliers, but the company set about making as much of the apparatus as possible themselves. A small workshop was started at Godalming, and Gerald Pritty was engaged to run it and develop production of metal fitments and parts for the Portabel and other departments of the company. The workshop became the nucleus of the present RFD

Systems Engineering Company. Meanwhile, if RFD could not make certain parts, they got them from the Midlands or went along Catteshall Lane to the engineering works of Joe Blackburn, who had been a close friend of Reginald Dagnall.

It was one of the foreign buyers (probably Denmark) who suggested that for their peacetime needs the trainer did not have to be portable; it might just as well be erected on a permanent site, in which case the dome could be made of wood or aluminium instead of the usual balloon fabric. RFD took the tip and offered the device either as a static dome trainer or as an inflatable dome.

By 1949 the chairman was able to report at the AGM that 'the anti-aircraft training apparatus is now in service with the British Army and is being used on an increasing scale by numerous forces abroad'. A year later the trainer had become one of the company's main products. The customers were Government departments and negotiations consequently took some time. In 1957, for example, the West German defence forces finally placed a contract after two years of preliminary discussions.

CHAPTER SEVEN

THE LIFERAFT GROWS UP

Note: During the 1950s the term 'liferaft' gradually came to be used instead of dinghy. The change was logical, for a dinghy is generally considered to be a craft which is propelled through the water by oars, paddles or outboard motor, whereas the liferaft is meant to stay in one place near the wrecked aircraft or ship that has necessitated its use, where it can be more easily spotted. From now onwards, therefore, such inflatables will be called liferafts in these pages, except where the word dinghy is specifically intended.

At first the company's sales of inflatables were affected by the disposal of surplus equipment by the Government to home and foreign buyers. The company accordingly went into the same line of business themselves. They bought up large numbers of surplus Q-type dinghies and after modifying them and fitting protective canopies, sold them to Iceland, which was the first country to appreciate the value of inflatable dinghies and liferafts for fishing boats.

While he was in Stockholm demonstrating the gunnery trainer, Bik took the opportunity to show the wartime K-type single-seater dinghy for fighter pilots to the Swedish Air Force, who gave RFD a contract. The company had no production dinghies to offer to begin with, so Bik bought up surplus RAF stock and after inspecting, renovating and testing the dinghies supplied them to Sweden as reconditioned models. Thousands more were sold to Switzerland.

Immediately after the war ended, RFD strengthened the management of the inflatable side of the business by enlisting a new executive technical director in the person of Major Sydney Nixon OBE, who came to the company from the Ministry of Aircraft Production, where he had been director of balloon production. Before the war he had been superintendent of the balloon development establishment at the airship factory at Cardington, so he was a man very much in the Dagnall tradition. Another recruit from the Ministry was Ronald Edwards, who had been working in the design branch and now joined RFD as technical salesman. Robert Bicknell, after a short spell with his pre-war employers, Power Boats, resumed his technical development work with RFD as a full-time member of the staff.

Bicknell had good connections in Sweden and started negotiations with the company's Swedish associates to get RFD towed targets made there for the Swedish Air Force in return for RFD making the Swedish winged target in Britain. A new company, RFD Air Targets Limited, was formed for this purpose in 1950. After extensive tests of the winged target had been carried out by the RAF and the Royal Navy, they decided to stick with the RFD towed target which had been one of Dagnall's earliest products and had been developed and improved over the years. The winged target project was abandoned after about 150 had been made.

With the post-war run-down of the RAF, it was obviously going to take some years before the Government contracts for liferafts would be resumed, so RFD concentrated on meeting the requirements of civil aviation, which were for liferafts with a larger carrying capacity than the 5-man and 7-man types that had sufficed for bombers during the war. By the time the Government offered RFD a contract to develop liferafts beyond the stage they had reached in 1945, the company were able to reply: 'Why don't you have a look at what we've been doing in the meantime?' Officials from the Ministry visited Godalming and found that, except for a few minor details which could easily be modified, the latest range of RFD liferafts met their requirements in full.

The main development since the war had been in providing protection from the elements by means of a wind-and-weather-proof canopy which greatly extended the period in which the occupants could be expected to survive. Canopies had been briefly used at the beginning of the war on the oval-shaped liferafts supplied to Imperial Airways for their flying boats on the London–New York service via the Azores. The canopy was supported by an automatically inflated arch-tube, but this was thought to be unsatisfactory because of its weight and bulk. For the canopy developed after the war the arch-tube was therefore discarded (for the time being) in favour of rigid arms pinioned around the top of the buoyancy chamber, over which the canopy was draped. The saving in weight meant that a 15-man liferaft with full protection was no heavier than an open 7-man liferaft, but in practice putting up the canopy manually—especially in rough weather—was beyond the capabilities of exhausted survivors.

A single-skin canopy had been used on the later type of one-man dinghy during the war. This was better than nothing, but did not provide much protection against the cold. Since the war RFD had been working on a much improved single-seat liferaft with an inflatable canopy which gave thermal protection. This was designed by Sidney Mitchell, who had joined the company in 1940 straight from school and had become Percy Williams' personal assistant and chief draughtsman in the experimental department. 'I was fired and taken on again once a week,' he recalls. (Williams was appointed chief designer of the aeronautical division on 1 January 1946, and died on 30 December the same year at the early age of forty-six).

A specimen single-seat liferaft with inflatable canopy was sent to the Institute of Aviation Medicine, who tested it in their laboratory and confirmed that there was a marked improvement in the degree of protection compared with the single-skin canopy. For the occupants of a liferaft the effect of 'wind chill' is particularly dangerous. At a temperature of 20°F, a 40mph wind has the same chilling effect as a temperature of minus 20°F with a wind of 5mph, and causes a loss of 1,400 calories an hour. In this instance the wind effect is equal to reducing the temperature by 40°F. It was now generally agreed that protection from exposure was even more important for survival than food and water.

Mitchell's single-seat liferaft was taken into service by the RAF as the SS Mark 3 and was called the Mark 5 for general use.

By 1950 liferafts with canopies were in such demand that the productive capacity of Godalming was insufficient to supply them. In 1952, with extended help from the Northern Ireland Government, a new factory based on an old bus station was opened at Dunmurry, near Belfast, which was—and with later extensions still is—the largest production plant in the RFD Group. After it had been running for a while the factory was put in the charge of Stanley Bell, who had been given a job with the company by Anton Bik when he disposed of his ball-point-pen interest. He did not stay long at Dunmurry and left RFD to join the rival company, Elliott Equipment, who were making liferafts in a nearby factory at Lisburn.

The Ministry then began to have grandiose ideas about the size of inflatables and asked RFD to design a 50-seater liferaft which would be suitable for the large RAF transports coming into service as well as for airliners. This resulted in an awkward-looking square contraption which RFD weren't too proud of, and they were further disconcerted when they found out that their old rivals, P. B. Cow, had been given the far more congenial assignment of producing a smaller and more practical 20-seater liferaft. Confronted with this anomaly, the Ministry agreed that RFD should be given the same opportunity, and in due course a circular 20-seater liferaft with double buoyancy chambers and rainwater catchments made its appearance.

In 1957 a 25/26-man aircraft liferaft was introduced and immediately found universal favour because it was lighter, less bulky and easier to stow than the 20-man type currently in use—an important consideration in the minds of airline operators with their constant search for increased payloads. In practical terms it meant that in a 100-complement aircraft only four rafts need be carried instead of five. The 25-man liferaft was also notable for the 're-invention' of the automatically inflated canopy, which had been tried out unsuccessfully in 1939. In its latest form it was no heavier than the old method of rigid arms holding up the canopy, and of course its automatic inflation was an enormous advantage. Inflatable arch-tubes were used in the 4-, 6- and 10-man liferafts; in the larger 12-, 15-, 20- and 26-man liferafts the canopy was supported by an inflatable centre strut.

The latest liferaft fulfilled the parallel requirements of providing a refuge for survivors of aircraft 'ditched' at sea and at the same time a shelter from intense heat or cold for the survivors of crash-landings in the desert or on the ice. In both conditions they would be able to live in the liferaft for some time until help arrived. It was not surprising that the first users were the Canadian Air Force, and it became an essential piece of equipment for airliners on flights across the North Pole. It was not long before the RFD 26-man liferaft was adopted by British Overseas Airways, Air France and most of the world's major airlines outside the United States. It was also taken up as standard equipment by RAF Transport Command.

The use of inflatable liferafts for ships had been rejected in 1948 by the Convention for the Safety of Life at Sea held by the United Nations Inter-Governmental Maritime Consultative Organisation. It was the general opinion in shipping circles that the risk of an accidental puncture made the inflatable liferaft unacceptable. However, on the strength of the satisfactory wartime experience with inflatables for air–sea rescue, RFD decided to go ahead with their plans to produce liferafts suitable for ships, using heavier and stronger fabrics than were either desirable or possible for liferafts carried by aircraft, where weight and stowage space are over-riding factors. After several years of development and trials, a range of 6-, 10- and 20-man liferafts (all with canopies) was produced and in September 1954 these were approved by the Ministry of Transport for use on trawlers and small merchant vessels sailing under British rules in British waters. Their value was convincingly demonstrated in April 1955 when the crew of the Grimsby trawler *Osako* were saved by RFD inflatables as she sank off the Faroe Islands in weather conditions that made it impossible to launch lifeboats. Meanwhile in Iceland, where Q-type dinghies had been carried in many fishing trawlers since the war, the compulsory use of inflatables for all fishing vessels, decreed in 1954, had been followed by the saving of three trawler crews in the space of twelve months.

The Icelandic experience was not lost on the British authorities and in 1956 they made the carriage of inflatables not merely acceptable but mandatory for all fishing craft. The effect was remarkable. Up to 1956 an average of 65 British fishermen had been lost every year—and as many as 112 in one day—whereas in the first three years following the mandatory carriage of liferafts not a single fisherman lost his life. In the first twelve months 73 were saved by liferafts.

In May 1958 the mandatory rules were extended to a few other types of vessel. Before long forty-five European and other countries had followed the lead of Iceland and the United Kingdom in adopting the use of inflatables for their trawlers and coasters operating in territorial waters.

Naval authorities had no inhibitions about using inflatables—they had seen them in action in air–sea rescue operations during the war. By 1955 the navies of Holland, Denmark, Belgium, Canada, Australia, New Zealand and South Africa had all approved RFD liferafts, and a prototype 20-seater had been supplied to the French Navy. The maritime version of the 25/26-man aviation liferaft was introduced in 1957 and brought contracts from the Swedish and German navies.

At home the Royal Navy had chosen the oval liferaft made by Elliott Equipment in preference to the RFD circular type, possibly because of reports of a tendency—long since overcome—of the earliest circular liferafts to spin. In their view the oval liferaft, having a greater maximum beam, was also less likely to capsize, though trials had shown that it was susceptible to excessive flexing unless inflatable thwarts were fitted to stiffen it. Perhaps the main advantages of the oval liferaft that appealed to the Navy were that it was easier to tow and to right after overturning. Its ventilation was also claimed to be superior. The Royal Navy were not alone in their preference, and when some shipowners expressed the same view in 1955, RFD produced a 20-seater oval liferaft in response.

One of the lessons learnt from various shipwrecks (notably the *Princess Victoria*, which sank in the Irish Sea in 1953 with the loss of 133 of the 172 people on board) was the need to provide life-saving equipment that could be launched at extreme angles of list in heavy seas. RFD solved this problem in 1958 when, with the co-operation of Schats Davits (the British subsidiary of a well-known Dutch company), they introduced the MC-type liferaft which could be lowered fully laden from a ship with a 60ft freeboard by means of a single-arm suspension davit, and automatically released. The MC-type liferaft was based on the standard RFD liferaft with dual buoyancy tubes and an inflatable centre strut for supporting the double-skinned canopy. The passengers boarded it at deck level by means of an apron which served the dual purpose of holding the liferaft firmly against the ship's side and providing a gangway. The liferaft was suspended in a substantially upright position by lifting straps as it was lowered over the side. One of its advantages was that it could be easily transported from one side of the ship to the other.

In a demonstration staged from the British Railways' ferry *Maid of Kent* at the Denny shipyard at Dumbarton in March that year, three fully manned MC-type liferafts were launched in quick succession from one Schats single-arm davit. It took only 2min 20sec for the liferaft to be water-borne from the time it was collected from the stowage position. In April 1959 live drops off a 70ft gantry were made to satisfy Ministry of Transport requirements and obtain type approval. Meanwhile, following wind-tunnel tests at Farnborough to prove the system's ability to operate in winds up to Force 9, a demonstration was given in *Clan McKay* on voyage from Hull to Aberdeen to show the suitability of the liferaft for abandoning ship when travelling through high winds.

Acceptance by the French Government was obtained after a live demonstration off a vessel at Le Havre, and in May 1960 the final test came when the davit-launched liferaft was formally approved by the delegates of the Inter-Governmental Consultative Organisation's Safety of Life at Sea Convention who saw it demonstrated at Tilbury Docks, London. (In the event, lack of parliamentary time delayed the ratification of the 1960 SOLAS Convention by the British Government, and inflatable liferafts were not made mandatory until May 1965. The full range of RFD liferafts was the first to receive approval under the new SOLAS regulations).

Inflatable liferafts were now approved on ships undertaking long international voyages—not in place of normal lifeboats, but complementing them to a maximum of 50 per cent. This was a sensible provision, because there was need for both. Lifeboats are extremely manoeuvrable and can move away from the area of danger relatively quickly. They are designed to stay afloat in the worst of seas, and they can be made fire-resistant. On the other hand they are at a disadvantage in certain conditions. For example, when a ship is listing heavily it is impossible to launch the conventional lifeboat, and in very rough seas it can be smashed to pieces against the side of a ship after it has been launched, whereas the inflatable liferaft harmlessly bounces off.

The 1960 SOLAS Convention stipulated standards of construction and materials that would enable liferafts to withstand exposure in all sea conditions for thirty days in temperatures ranging from minus 30°C to 66°C. RFD had anticipated such requirements several years earlier in the development of their liferaft by mooring prototypes for months on end in the Atlantic, where they were monitored by the ocean weather ships.

For some time after the war the fabric used for liferafts continued to be made of cotton—in fact, the cotton specified for the barrage balloons in the late 1930s. It had a high strength-to-weight ratio and was made in 2-ply and 3-ply forms, both with one 'bias' ply laid at 45° to the straight to augment resistance to tearing. In the 1950s the even better strength-to-weight ratio of continuous-filament synthetic textiles made it obvious that if they could be successfully proofed, reductions in weight and thickness for a given strength could be expected, and this turned out to be so. By 1957 many liferafts for a large civil airline had been made with a synthetic textile. (Twelve years later some of these liferafts, either in store or in aircraft, were still in first-rate condition, and synthetic fabrics were introduced for marine liferafts.) Synthetic textiles also had the important advantage over cotton of being

86

immune from attacks of mould. This had always been a worry, because although a preventative chemical had been used for cotton fabrics, its effectiveness was limited.

The RFD circular liferafts of the 1960s were the culmination of intensive development since the war and incorporated the lessons in design and equipment learnt from continuous trials and customer experience. Except for the single-seater, they had double buoyancy tubes for extra safety, a double-skin floor and an integral canopy. Climbing into them from the sea was made as easy as possible by webbing ladders and, on the 12-man size upwards, inflatable boarding ramps. Hauling-in lines were provided for those already inside to give a hand to survivors still in the water, and a lifeline inside gave a hand-hold. Water-activated cells underneath the floor automatically illuminated a lamp on top of the canopy so that the raft could be located, and at the same time gave some light to the occupants inside. A drogue could be streamed as a sea-anchor to control the rate of drift. The positions of the safety knife, rescue line, quoit and topping-up valves were shown by illustrated labels. A radio aerial was incorporated in a sleeve. Two tubes for rain catchment off the canopy were supplied, and emergency packs contained rations and further equipment. An equipment bag contained a water-proof torch and spare battery and bulbs, leak stoppers, repair kit, a spare sea-anchor and a table of life-saving signals. A pair of paddles was packed with sponge-rubber protection.

The value of the fully equipped canopied liferaft in helping ship-wrecked mariners to survive in extreme cold was illustrated in March 1962 when the *Marconia* struck a reef and sank within six minutes off Unga Island in the Aleutians. The crew of ten took to their liferaft and were soon enjoying a temperature of 70°F on a freezing Arctic night. Thanks to the protection of their liferaft they survived.

'Feed-back' from users indicated that the rot-proof canvas valise in which the liferaft was packed was liable to get knocked about on deck, so in 1957 RFD produced a rigid glass-fibre container which retained all the advantages of automatic release enjoyed by the conventional valise while at the same time effectively protecting the fabric from the possibility of damage. (To recapitulate, a tug on the painter after the container or valise was dropped overboard released carbon dioxide gas from a cylinder situated on the underside of the liferaft, whereupon the liferaft inflated and the container or valise burst open. The liferaft was fully inflated and ready for its life-saving duties within 30 seconds of touching the water.)

Although the canvas (later neoprene-coated nylon) valise continued to be made, the majority of liferafts were supplied in containers that could be stowed in tiers or multiple racks capable of operating with a list of 15°. Cradles were supplied to fit the various sizes of containers for installation at the ship's rail. This method helped to comply with the 1960 SOLAS Convention requirement for liferafts to be stowed in such a way that the ship must be evacuated within 30 minutes. At a demonstration held on Loch Long in July 1957 a mass launching of nineteen RFD 20-man liferafts in valises took place from the Caledonian Steam Packet Company's car-and-passenger ferry MV *Glen Sannox*, which carried thirty-eight liferafts altogether.

Under the 1960 SOLAS Convention the weight of a liferaft in its container or valise was limited to 400lb in order that two people could launch it over the side. It was difficult to keep below this limit with the larger rafts, one way of saving weight being to substitute de-salting apparatus for one-third of the tins of drinking water carried. Containers and valises had to be robust as well as light, and able to withstand drop-testing from 60ft. (Later this was to be increased to 120ft for dropping from oil-rigs.)

The next step was to ensure that the container or valise would be automatically released from its cradle in the event of its becoming submerged before it could be manually released. This was achieved by a hydrostatic mechanism bolted to the ship's deck and secured to the webbing straps holding the container on the cradle. Disasters so sudden that manual launching of liferafts was impossible were most likely to occur with small ships and the hydrostatic release mechanism soon proved its worth when it saved the lives of the crews of two trawlers, *Orion* and *Ajax*, in New Zealand. By the end of 1959 reports of rescues with all kinds of RFD liferafts were coming in so regularly that as many as fifty in a month were not unusual.

In 1957 the company helped the RAF in designing a Mark 3 version of the wartime Lindholme rescue gear. This comprised three cylindrical containers, one with a 10-man liferaft and the other two with supplies (food, dry clothing, signalling equipment, etc) which were dropped to the leeward of survivors afloat in liferafts remote from rescue ships. The containers were linked together by floating cord with a spread of 550 metres, compared with the 365 metres of the wartime version. On striking the water the 10-man liferaft was automatically inflated and burst out of its container. The equipment was put into service with all

RAF aircraft, including Shackletons operating at speeds from 140 to 160 knots, both for bomb-bay and fuselage dropping. It was not long before it was being supplied to the Australian, New Zealand, German, Malaysian, Indian and Muscat Governments.

The latest Lindholme gear was instrumental in saving many lives when the Greek cruise liner *Lakonia* caught fire in mid-Atlantic on 23 December 1963 with the loss of 128 of her 1,032 passengers. Four of the lifeboats were damaged in the fire and two overturned when they were launched. The 1960 SOLAS Convention had not been implemented and there were no liferafts on board. Lindholme gear was dropped by RAF Shackletons operating from Cornwall, Ireland and Gibraltar, without which the loss of life would have been even greater.

By the end of the 1950s the number of British shipping companies using RFD liferafts had grown to over a hundred. Export orders increased from many parts of the world, and in three countries subsidiary companies were established to further the manufacture, maintenance and repair of the company's products. These were RFD (Canada) Limited in Montreal, RFD (Australia) Co Pty Limited in Melbourne, and RFD (Africa) Pty Limited in Germiston.

The idea of organising RFD's European business on a corporate scale had been in Anton Bik's mind for some time before the Treaty of Rome was signed on 25 March 1957 as a prelude to the establishment of the European Economic Community a year later. In fact it was in 1955 that Bik's ideas crystallised in the formation of RFD Europa Limited to act as a holding company for local RFD companies set up initially in Holland, Sweden and France. Further companies in Norway and Germany followed soon afterwards. The largest shareholding in the company was held by RFD; each of the local companies had 10 per cent holdings, and Bik himself—at the request of the local companies—was also allotted 10 per cent. RFD had a 60 per cent holding in each of the local companies, which were represented by individual directors on the board of RFD Europa.

In France an arrangement was made with Zodiac, the leading manufacturer of inflatable dinghies, for a cross-licensing agreement whereby RFD made Zodiac dinghies in England and Zodiac made RFD dinghies in France. M. Desanges, the head of Zodiac, was made a director of RFD Europa. Actually, RFD had produced dinghies with outboard motors for some time before they realised that the similar Zodiac dinghy was covered by a patent. (Desanges unhappily died soon afterwards and the subsequent financial settlement of the cross-licensing arrangement was unsatisfactory from RFD's point of view.)

The Zodiac inflatable with outboard motor formed the basis of the RFD crash rescue unit, which went into service at specific civil airports and RAF stations at home and abroad. The unit was designed for use in disasters at airfields adjoining shallow water or near the coast, and consisted of a trailer on which was stowed a Zodiac boat, a searchlight and two RFD liferafts.

One good effect of RFD Europa was that it was largely responsible for keeping RFD in the inflatable-boat business. The spin-off came in 1963 when, after a period of co-operation and trials, RFD inflatable boats were approved by the Royal National Lifeboat Institution for the new inshore rescue service they had been planning for some time. An order for a hundred boats was received and they went into service all round the British Isles. The RFD inshore rescue boat was 15ft 6in long and had a crew of two. It was made of neoprene-proofed nylon and was powered by a 40hp outboard engine that gave it a speed of well over 20 knots. Half the fleet was later equipped with VHF radio telephone.

The first rescue was reported from Aberystwyth in August 1964 when three people and a dog were saved, and by 1968 some 1,500 people had been rescued by the Inshore Rescue Service—not to mention countless yachts and small boats retrieved and towed to safety. The original idea was to operate the service only in the summer months, but the scheme was so successful that it was decided to keep twenty stations open all the year round. A similar scheme was started in the Channel Islands by the St John's Ambulance Service and their RFD inflatable boats made many rescues round the rocky coasts.

The management of RFD underwent some radical changes during the post-war years. Three directors died in the early months of 1951. First Edward Shrapnell-Smith, who had been chairman since the company's inception, collapsed and died while making a speech in Kent on 8 April, and within the space of five weeks he was followed by Arthur Johnson, who had supervised the flotation of the company in 1936, and Major Sydney Nixon, who had been a director for six years. The latter's brother, Sir Norman Nixon, who had recently retired as governor of the Bank of Egypt, offered to take his place as a non-executive director and was gladly accepted, for by this time there were only two directors

(*above*) The RFD factory at Godalming today. On the right can be seen the dome gunnery trainer marketed by RFD Systems Engineering and the Canberra bomber which is in continual use for demonstrating the RFD aircraft recovery system; (*below*) all that was left of the Godalming factory after the fire on the night of 17/18 August 1954. The cause was never discovered

STATICHUTE

LIFT WEBS

OUTER PACK COVER

OUTER PACK
FLAPS TIED
TOGETHER
WITH NYLON
CORD HERE

HARNESS

STATIC LINE

"D" RING IS ATTACHED
TO STRONG-POINT IN
A/C BEFORE JUMP
IS MADE

The GQ Statichute, designed by Raymond Quilter and James Gregory for Britain's first airborne forces in 1940, was the most effective static-line parachute ever made and continued in production for more than 20 years left. Anton Bik did not think it was desirable to be chairman as well as managing director, so Norman Hulbert took the chair in succession to Shrapnell-Smith. The directors remained only three in number till June 1955, when John Rawsthorn MC, who had known RFD well for many years as joint managing director of Mandelbergs, the textile-proofing company, joined the board.

In the following year Sir Norman Hulbert (he was knighted in 1955) set about gaining complete control of the RFD Company. Without telling the other directors he submitted notices to the registrar for the appointment of three additional directors to be appointed at the annual general meeting to be held on 28 June 1956. Since he did this four days after the notice convening the meeting had been posted, it was too late for his proposal to be included in the notice. His plan was that the proxy forms of shareholders who could not attend (which in most cases would be naturally made out in his favour as chairman of the company) could be used to dismiss the present board and vote in the new directors.

As soon as the other directors found out, they held a special board meeting at Claridge's on 15 June and steps were taken to ensure that Hulbert's stratagem was circumvented at the AGM.

Not in the least put out, Hulbert thereupon wrote to the shareholders and asked them to support a requisition for an extraordinary general meeting to be called to elect the three additional directors in order to provide fresh blood on the board and improve the company's position. (He did not, of course, explain that his true reason for wanting the new directors was to gain complete control of the company.)

This move was immediately countered by a letter from the company to the shareholders pointing out that Hulbert's letter had been issued without the knowledge of the managing director and the other directors. They unanimously opposed the appointment of additional directors. A fuller letter was sent out on 13 September recording the events that had led to the present disagreement.

While this was going on Hulbert was voted out of the chair by the board and Bik, while continuing as managing director, was installed in his place as a temporary measure.

But Hulbert was still full of fight. On 20 September he wrote to the company enclosing 673 forms of requisition, representing more than 10 per cent of the share capital, which was sufficient for the extra-ordinary general meeting to be called in accordance with the articles of association. A few days later the directors took the precaution of enlarging the board by appointing Gerald Pritty, who had been largely responsible for organising the manufacture of components for the gunnery trainer, as an executive director.

With the notice convening the meeting, the board sent a long letter going over the background and ending by an appeal to shareholders to vote against two of the three nominations—Major Leonard Garland MC and Percival Wheeler; the third nominee, Philip Lucas, had withdrawn his nomination on 30 September. (Lucas was furious when an item appeared in the press during the Farnborough Air Show stating that he had agreed to join RFD, when in fact no firm commitment had been made and he had not even met the present directors.)

By now letters from Hulbert and the board were landing thick and fast in shareholders' letter boxes. Hulbert added to the stack with a letter stating that his sole object was to strengthen the board, and he went on to make a long and vindictive attack on Bik and the way he ran the company as managing director.

The company immediately came back with another long letter rebutting Hulbert's accusations and also his claim—which was manifestly incorrect—that he had told the directors about his intention to nominate three more directors before doing anything about it.

Eventually the extraordinary general meeting took place at the Connaught Rooms on 25 October. Hulbert was confident that he would win the day with the support he had received from the City, but to his dismay the voting went heavily against him. In both cases the votes cast against the appointment of new directors were almost double those cast in favour.

The company were soon able to find a permanent chairman in the person of Henry (later Sir Henry) Spencer, the managing director of Richard Thomas & Baldwins, the big steel company, who was an RFD shareholder and had approached Bik after the extraordinary general meeting with an offer to help in any way he could. He was invited to join the board and was made a director on 8 November, being appointed chairman shortly afterwards.

On the same day the board was greatly strengthened by the appointment of Philip Lucas as a non-executive director. On meeting him for the first time, Bik had immediately realised his potential value to the company and in due course he was invited to join the board now that the Hulbert fracas was out of the way. (In conversation it transpired that when Hulbert originally approached Lucas through his stockbroker, he had offered him the job of deputy managing director.) Following a distinguished career as chief test pilot of Hawker Aircraft during the war—he was awarded the George Medal for bravery in bringing down safely an aircraft on test when it began to break up— Lucas had been made director and general manager of the company in 1946 before joining de Havilland Aircraft as technical sales manager in the following year. With de Havilland's consent Lucas now accepted the RFD invitation, and his wide and close contacts in the aircraft industry at home and abroad proved to be extremely useful to the company (though there were times when he felt that these contacts were not as fully utilised by RFD as they might have been, especially in France and Sweden).

In the new year of 1957 the company wrote to the shareholders once more, informing them that they had received a communication from a firm of accountants claiming to represent 'a small committee of shareholders'. As the directors had no knowledge of a mandate by the general body of shareholders to this or any other committee, they had declined to recognise the committee or to disclose to it or its members any matters affecting the internal management of the company.

Even then Hulbert did not give up. He wrote to Bik, emphasising that he was not concerned with the activities of the committee (though he seemed to be remarkably well informed about it) and went on to ask Bik to meet him to discuss the company's affairs, adding that he would be particularly interested to know what his attitude would be if he received a bid for 51 per cent of the company's shares.

A reply was sent by the board, signed by the Secretary, stating that they had considered his letter but saw no reason why such a meeting should take place. If the directors received a take-over bid from a responsible source, it would of course be considered by them in the ordinary way. And there the matter rested.

All these upheavals seemed to have had an unsettling effect through-out the company, resulting in unfulfilled orders and complaints of poor product quality. The deflationary policy of the Government, coupled with a recession in the shipping industry and intensified competition, all tended to reduce the company's marine business, and the net profit fell from a peak figure of £147,637 in 1955 to £119,854 in 1958.

It was lucky for RFD that just at that moment events in another industry in a different part of the country brought about a change in their own fortunes. The critical position in the Lancashire cotton trade

95

forced RFD to look to the security of their textile sources, and at the same time the Perseverance Mill Company, their main suppliers, found it expedient to become part of a larger group. An arrangement that met both requirements was satisfactorily concluded in 1959, but before we recount the details of that agreement let us look at the origin and development of RFD's sturdy new ally.

CHAPTER EIGHT

A POWERFUL REINFORCEMENT

In 1901 Herbert Noble, the son of a mill manager at Great Harwood, near Blackburn, grew bored with working for his father and bought a run-down old mill at Padiham, five miles away. The name of the mill was Perseverance, but this was seldom used. The mill was always referred to locally as 'Old Shah', though nobody to this day has ever been able to explain why. (There were nicknames for everything in Lancashire in those days—houses and workplaces as well as people. Commercial Mill, for example, was called 'Old Brooks's', while another mill was called 'Catoile' because it had a cat-hole in the front door for the mill cat. Few people would have been able to tell you its real name.)

Herbert Noble was able to launch out on his own as a result of a successful gamble. He went to the Liverpool cotton exchange one day and bought a large amount of cotton at a very low price and sold it very quickly on a rising market. With the proceeds he was able to become the owner of a mill with 706 looms at the age of thirty-two.

George Whitaker, a retired Perseverance Mill weaving manager, described the workforce to me in these words:

> Dob Pickles was the weaving manager, Owd Potter the engine tenter and boilerman. George Leedham was the head cloth-looker, G. Kearsley the warehouse manager and book-keeper. The tacklers were Owd Ned Davies and half a dozen others. Weavers who come to mind were the O'Hare family, the Merlins, the Brindleys, and Billy Grime and his family.
>
> Billy was the knocker-up. His day started around 4 am and he used a cane with a wire on the end to rap on the bedroom windows. Everybody paid for this service and it got them to work on time. The working day was 6 am to 5.30 pm Monday to Friday and finish 11.30 am on Saturday. There was no room for shirkers—everybody had to work to live. The Governor travelled daily to Manchester for orders and had faith in his workforce to give him the goods he booked.

At first Herbert Noble came to work in a gig from his house in Warley Road. Although he had a groom named Froggett, he insisted on driving himself, but on arrival at the mill he could never get the pony to stop going round and round in circles until Froggett jumped down and held its head. In a few years the gig was replaced by his first motor-car, driven by a chauffeur named Lockley who astonished everyone at the mill by turning up on the first day in an immaculate maroon livery, complete with peaked cap.

As soon as he got 'Old Shah' in working order again, Herbert Noble looked around for ways of doing more business. In 1906 he found what he wanted in the Albion Room and Power Company, the title of which said exactly what it was—a leasing company (common in Lancashire at that time) which provided room and power for weaving and other textile companies to carry on their trade without having to invest capital for those purposes.

The Albion Room and Power premises were too large for one weaving company to occupy, so they were divided into two. Herbert Noble, who was a director of the leasing company, took over one half of the premises and called it the Albion Mill, operating as a branch of Perseverance Mill, which continued to be the name of the company. The other half was occupied by the Church Street Manufacturing Company and was called the Church Street Mill. It was run by a man named Thomas Noble, who was not related to Herbert. Albion Mill had 794 looms and Church Street Mill 810, the average cost of a loom being about £7. Four years later an extension shed was added to the Albion Mill to take 376 looms. Tape frames, winding frames and beaming frames made up the rest of the plant, together with a 1,200hp horizontal twin-cylinder steam engine and two Lancahire coal-fired boilers.

The early production of the Perseverance and Albion mills was mostly Indian mulls and other cotton cloths of ordinary construction woven from good quality American or Egyptian yarns. The Indian cloth was used for making saris and was sometimes interwoven with gold thread. This was the time when India was the largest piece-goods export market for the British cotton industry—in the years from 1909 to 1913 it took nearly one-third of the total production, which reached an all-time peak volume.

The outbreak of war in 1914 brought a demand for better-class cloths—aeroplane fabric and other high-reed and pick cloths. Large orders for aeroplane fabric were received from the United States, marking the beginning of a business that was to continue without a break (though sometimes reduced to a trickle) right through the interval between the two world wars. American aeroplanes were traditionally covered with a cotton fabric (the British used linen), for which the native yarn was not suitable. Herbert Noble was quick to supply the greatly expanded American aeroplane production with fabrics made of Egyptian cotton, which was ideal for the work. Perseverance Mill was also one of America's chief suppliers of fabric for balloons—as of course it was to Airships Limited and other airship factories at home. By the end of the war Perseverance Mill had begun to concentrate on the production of industrial fabric weaving.

The return of peace in 1918 saw the beginning of a marked decline in the British cotton trade with India, brought on largely by the competition of low-wage local mills. The crowning blow was Gandhi's programme of non-violence and non-co-operation in 1920 which included the boycott of British manufactures. By 1924 British world-wide exports of cotton piece-goods were down to 69 per cent of the 1910–13 average.

In 1921 a World Cotton Conference was organised in New Orleans and the British Government offered to pay the fares of delegates from home. Herbert Noble was the odd man out and insisted on paying his own fare so that he could be free to do what he liked while he was in the States. In fact, he took the opportunity to form an association with W. Harris Thurston, a man of great drive and considerable charm, who became the sole importer of Perseverance Mill products. One section of the early American trade that was to have enormous potentiality for Perseverance Mill was the supply of fabric for typewriter ribbons. This built up to the point when Perseverance became the biggest maker and exporter of typewriter fabrics to America before the war. In those days typewriter ribbons were made of cotton—the success story of the nylon fabric ribbon, for computers as well as typewriters, belongs to a later period.

But the most important immediate consequence of the arrangement made with Thurston was the contract to supply the fabric of the ZR-1, the US Navy's first airship, better known perhaps as the *Shenandoah*. The design of the airship was based on the German Zeppelin L49, which had run out of petrol while cruising over France at 20,000ft during the war and was captured intact. (The sister Zeppelin L45 on the same flight also ran out of petrol but was burnt by the crew on landing.) The ZR-1 flew for the first time on 4 September 1923 and eight days later it cruised majestically over New York. Perseverance Mill still have a framed photograph of the occasion issued by W. Harris Thurston & Co Inc in which the caption claims 'We are the largest manufacturers of cotton aircraft fabric in America. Mechanical cloth specialists and producers of fine and light cotton cloths.'

Herbert Noble was too much of a realist to protest about Thurston's claim. All that mattered to him was that Perseverance Mill supplied the fabric for the ZR-1. As a footnote, it might be added that the *Shenandoah*, after a career of propaganda flights and a few naval exercises, broke up in a thunderstorm on the night of 2 September 1925, killing 14 of its crew of 43.

But American faith in airships was undiminished by the fate of the ZR-1 and the previous disaster of the ZR-2, which had been bought in England as the R.38 and broke in two during a trial flight at Hull before it could be delivered to America. In 1928 the Goodyear–Zeppelin partnership put forward two airships, the ZR-4 (the *Akron*) and the ZR-5 (the *Macon*) for which Perseverance Mill supplied the fabric through the agency of W. Harris Thurston. Both airships were adapted to act as airborne hangars for four aeroplanes. The *Akron* flew for the first time on 21 September 1931. Eighteen months later she headed out to sea from Lakenhurst base and ran into the worst storm for ten years, never to be seen again. There were three survivors from her complement of 73 crew and passengers. The *Macon* first flew in 1933 and was lost two years later.

Meanwhile Perseverance Mill had supplied the vast amounts of fabric used in the construction of the R.100 and R.101 airships at home. Both were launched in the second half of 1929. Herbert Noble and his eldest son Alan were among the select party of guests invited to travel in the R.101 on its maiden flight to India, but they decided they were too busy running their mill in Lancashire to spare the time for such an extended jaunt, and declined the invitation. That rushed, ill-prepared and consequently fatal flight ended on the night of 4–5 October 1930 when the great airship, losing height in the darkness over France, crashed into a low hillside near Beauvais at 02.05 hours, killing or mortally injuring 48 of the 54 persons on board.

But we have flown ahead of our story. Reverting to Herbert Noble's visit to the 1921 World Cotton Convention, this was in effect the start

Thousands of Allied airmen owed their lives to rescue dinghies and boats during the war. Here an airborne lifeboat (developed by Uffa Fox) is dropped from an aircraft with three parachutes to the crew of an American Flying Fortress bomber which has come down in the sea. The airborne lifeboat had self-righting buoyancy chambers supplied by RFD which automatically inflated on splash-down and prevented it from overturning

Sir Raymond Quilter's boundless energy extended beyond the operations of GQ Parachutes to such different outlets as bomb disposal (in a civilian capacity) during the war and skin-diving, which held a tremendous fascination for him. Lady Quilter has continued to take an active interest in the Group since his early death in 1959

The late Airey Neave MP, visiting the RFD factory at Dunmurry in Northern Ireland in 1957, when he was joint parliamentary secretary to the Ministry of Transport and Civil Aviation. With him is Anton van Beugen Bik, the RFD managing director. In the smaller picture he is seen inspecting one of the RFD liferafts made at Dunmurry

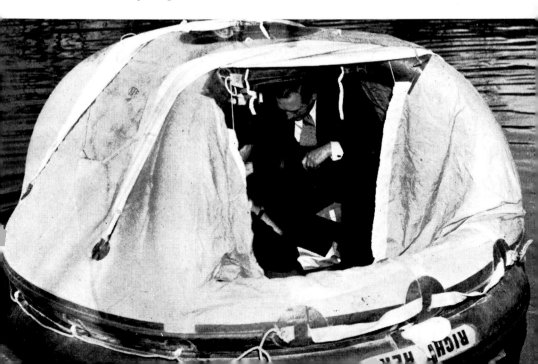

Air brake parachutes: (*above*) the 24-litre Napier-Railton raced by the late John Cobb
before the war was acquired by GQ Parachutes for the development of the air brake
parachute. Raymond Quilter drove it himself at Dunsfold aerodrome to test the re-
traction of the parachute into its housing when the speed was reduced; (*below*) a 45ft ring-
slot brake parachute being streamed from a Handley Page Victor bomber during landing.
The smallest size made was 7ft 6in in diameter and was fitted to the Folland Gnat jet
trainer

of Perseverance Mill's peacetime trade in America, which became so important that at one stage the mill accounted for no less than 17 per cent of the total British cotton exports to the United States. On his twice-yearly voyages across the Atlantic Herbert Noble always made money in gambling on the ship's daily run, so the company never had to pay a penny for his fare. His reputation for luck was enhanced by the story told by an influential American friend who ran the New York cotton exchange. One day at the races together he asked Herbert what he was going to back. Herbert took the newspaper and marked five horses—and they all won.

The American trade continued to be done through W. Harris Thurston until 1928, when the American got into financial difficulties. He was extricated by the assistance of Herbert Noble, with whom he had built up a close but apparently indeterminate business relationship. The failure of Thurston's company caused Perseverance Mill to sustain a heavy loss—the only time it has done so in its long history—and it was in turn greatly helped by Martin's Bank.

There were two ways of meeting, or rather circumventing, the decline of the Lancashire cotton trade and Perseverance Mill employed both. The first was by accentuating their emphasis on special fabrics, like typewriter-ribbon fabric and sail-cloth (Perseverance wove the *Endeavour's* balloon jib sail for the America's Cup races in the 1930s) instead of attempting to compete in the mass apparel market, and the second was by raising productivity. It was therefore a timely coincidence that at this critical period Herbert Noble's energy was reinforced by the vigorous new blood of his sons as they entered the business. Alan and Eric now set to work on the productivity problem, while Frank, the third son, was sent to learn the sales side of the company's business in the Manchester office. A small building adjacent to Albion Mill was purchased and rebuilt, and thirty to forty box looms, working on three shifts, were installed on the ground floor. (Perseverance Mill were pioneers of three-shift working in Lancashire.) By the late 1920s six looms were being worked by one weaver.

The years 1930–31 saw the start of silk and rayon weaving. This brought a new spirit into the Mill; it was almost a new industry and it appealed to the young workforce, whose average age was between seventeen and twenty-seven years. Half-a-dozen silk looms were installed in the 'old laundry'—two of them French, two Swiss, and two British looms copied from foreign designs. These looms gave such a

105

good account of themselves that a further thirty-two were bought. Then, largely due to the lessons learnt at Perseverance Mill, a new part-French, part-Lancashire silk loom was produced by Butterworth & Dickinson and proved an outstanding success—it was to continue in production till the early 1970s. In 1934 the box looms were transferred to the Extension and new ones added, the whole shed going over to three-shift working.

By the mid-thirties the fourth member of the Noble family, Brian, who had learnt to weave in the mill on leaving school, was joining in experiments with pick counters on the looms to obtain better output. Up to that time the weavers were paid by piece work, but with the installation of pick counters the system was changed to payment for every thousand picks. The tackler was paid so much for every pound that a weaver earned.

In 1935 the company invited Associated Industrial Consultants to submit a project for still further increasing the efficiency of the mill. (The name was a new one to hide the identity of the Bedaux Organisation, whose plan for incentive payment by results had caused a great deal of opposition when it had been introduced a few years earlier, especially at the Wolsey textile factory at Leicester and the motor components firm of Joseph Lucas in Birmingham.) Two inspectors arrived at Padiham and worked out a system based on a starting-point wage of £3 a week and a bonus for every hundred thousand picks that came off a section of the looms. The incentive for the overlooker was to keep his looms running so that they produced the maximum number of picks which gave the operatives the maximum bonus—on which he got a percentage.

Three members of the Perseverance Mill were detailed to work with the inspectors and put the plan into effect—Brian Noble, H. Beardsell and George Whitaker. This was not achieved without some initial opposition, but in the end, with the team-work and co-operation of all concerned, the company benefited by getting higher output and the workforce earned more pay.

Industrial relations presented few problems at Perseverance Mill. The only strike did not concern the company—the tacklers (overlookers) came out in sympathy with strikers at another mill. It lasted for three days, but work was not resumed for the rest of the week. The tackler was a skilled mechanic who could put anything right that went wrong with the looms, and he could produce any particular type of fabric that could be made by the loom. In the case of the Lancashire loom this meant eighty different sorts of cloth, which enabled the company to supply special fabrics that other people did not want to make.

John Mannion, one of the leading trade unionists in the company, summed up industrial relations at the mill:

> The management at Perseverance are down-to-earth men. They're not absentees; they're on the job as you might say. We understand each other's language. In other words we seem to be able to sense each and all's problem. Many's the time when with Mister Eric, he has said Aye and I've said No. We've cooled off a bit and then we'd get it sorted out in the end.

But the drive for efficient production did not detract from the company's boast that it produced the finest and lightest cotton cloths. This was demonstrated in a striking fashion when a special lawn handkerchief was made for the Royal Family by Norman Hartnell at the time of the Coronation of King George VI in 1937. The yarn—Sea Island cotton, the longest grown anywhere in the world—was spun by Thomas Oliver & Sons in Cheshire and woven by Perseverance Mill in Lancashire before being bleached, dyed, rolled (hemmed) and embroidered in Northern Ireland. The result was undoubtedly the finest cotton lawn ever made. On a visit to the United States shortly afterwards Brian Noble talked to the president of some American mills who extolled the extraordinary quality of his company's products. Brian pulled the handkerchief out of his pocket, put it on his face, and blew. The handkerchief went almost up to the ceiling. The American was amazed: 'His eyes came out like organ stops, and when he examined it he said he would never have believed it possible to make anything so fine'.

In recounting this incident Brian Noble added: 'Whatever we've made, we've always been at the top end, the connoisseur's market.'

And just to show their versatility, Perseverance Mills also produced very thick cotton fabrics of the highest quality for the Mount Everest expeditions before (and after) the war.

The decline in the British overseas trade in cotton piece-goods accelerated during the 1930s and by 1938 the exports of cotton piece-goods were only 20 per cent of the 1910–13 average. In the following year the preliminary steps were taken to reorganise the industry by the establishment of the Cotton Industry Board.

The threat of war brought a revival in balloon cloths, which the company had supplied continuously to the Air Ministry and the American Government since the First World War. Perseverance Mill had held a large stock when the disasters at home and in the United States put an end to the giant airship, and this was available when barrage balloons began to be manufactured in large numbers by RFD and Dunlop in 1937. But the stock was soon exhausted and production of balloon fabric was resumed. For the rest of the war Perseverance Mill was one of the leading producers of balloon, parachute and similar fabrics in Lancashire, sometimes having to use yarns supplied by the Government that the company would not have accepted in peacetime.

Immediately after the war the decision was taken to concentrate the company's production in one place, so weaving was ended at 'Old Shah' and transferred to the part of the Albion Room & Power premises that had been recently taken over from the previous occupants. The whole site—the original Albion Mill (now called No 1) with its Extension, and the Church Street Mill (latterly called Danes Mill) which now became known as Albion No 2—was operated as Perseverance Mill with a combined capacity of more than 1,600 cotton looms and 256 semi-silk looms. The opportunity was taken to install air-conditioning in most of the premises as well as fluorescent lighting, which greatly improved the working conditions.

Working conditions were always on the agenda of the works council set up in 1946, the main object being for the workers themselves, together with management, to control absenteeism and general behaviour. In John Mannion's phrase: 'Many useful subjects were discussed, for the benefit of all.' The end of the year saw the end of Saturday working and the introduction of the five-day week, a move welcomed by management as much as by the operatives. As Eric Noble remarked: 'Saturday never did produce cheap fabric.'

On 1 January 1947 the coal mines came under the control of the National Coal Board. Perseverance Mill celebrated the occasion by completing the conversion of its boilers to oil firing. By doing so they escaped the consequences of the cut in coal supplies to 65 per cent of regular deliveries resulting from the coal strike that winter, which caused spasmodic stoppages in many Lancashire mills. In any case coal deliveries were appallingly uncertain, whereas there was a guaranteed twenty-four-hour service of oil deliveries.

With ever-increasing competition in the world textile trade after the war, Perseverance Mill took up once more the pursuit of higher productivity. A newcomer to the family team who was to make his mark in the future—Jeremy Higham, the son of Herbert Noble's daughter Hilda—arrived on the scene in 1945 and worked with George Whitaker for six months putting in larger boxes on the Lancashire looms. The manning rate went up from eight to twelve and eventually from twelve to twenty looms per weaver.

When manning reached that stage a few years later, it was time to think of automation. But the Nobles did not rush their fences. With typical Lancashire caution they began by buying twenty second-hand LF Northrop automatics from Australia. When these had been tested and found satisfactory they bought another twenty RB Northrop silk automatics, again second-hand, and these formed a sound basis for further expansion.

In 1949 the company suffered the grievous loss of its founder, Herbert Noble, who died on 29 October in his eightieth year. A truly remarkable man, he left behind him a splendid business which he had steered through periods of crisis in the cotton trade that had decimated the Lancashire mills. And he left behind him, too, a remarkable family, in whose hands the future of Perseverance Mill was assured. Alan, the eldest, now assumed his father's mantle as head of the business, and was ably supported by Eric who ran the production side of the mill, Frank who sold the mill's output from the Manchester office, and Brian who started at Perseverance Mill before serving in the war, after which he moved to the nearby Prospect Manufacturing Company, one of two separately run mills (the second was Parkside) which by this time were also owned by the Noble family. Finally, Jeremy Higham, Herbert's grandson, had recently joined Perseverance Mill as the first of another generation.

The sales office in Manchester had been an important branch of Perseverance Mill from the beginning, growing from a simple 'calling shop' used by the salesmen from the mill to two offices and a warehouse when shipments of typewriter-ribbon fabric to the United States started in the early 1920s. Leslie Wright, who joined the office in 1928 on leaving school, remembers that the standard case contained eight pieces, each 300 yards in length, making a total of 2,400 yards. The biggest shipment was ninety-nine cases. The cases were shipped on alternate weeks by Cunard and White Star, who competed for the Atlantic trade from Liverpool. After several moves the office and warehouse settled at 12 Atan Street in 1938 (staying there for the next thirty years till they were closed and moved to Padiham in 1968).

There was a growing tendency in the 1950s for cotton mills to enlarge their scope by processing man-made fibres. This was the course taken at Perseverance Mill, but in many mills the change-over was complete and they ceased to produce cotton fabrics. Indeed, by 1960 the UK had become the world's largest importer of cotton fabrics, due partly to the low wages in India, Pakistan and Hongkong and also because these countries had duty-free access to the British domestic market.

Faced with this contraction of the cotton industry, RFD decided to make sure of their main source of supply of the woven fabrics essential for the manufacture of liferafts. Negotiations were begun with Perseverance Mill to see whether some closer arrangement could be made. Perseverance Mill were not unwilling, because in the uncertain state of the Lancashire cotton trade they would benefit from being part of a more widely based group. Furthermore, being part of a larger group would make their shares marketable, something they had always wanted but had not been able to achieve as a small company. They had known and worked with RFD since the early days of Reginald Dagnall, and now 37 per cent of their trade was done with Godalming. With goodwill on both sides, the negotiations went smoothly.

An extraordinary general meeting of RFD Company Limited was held at Grosvenor House, Park Lane, London on 30 September 1959 at which the acquisition of the undertaking and certain assets of the Perseverance Mill Company Limited was approved, the purchase consideration being 1,000,000 shares of two shillings each in RFD, for which purpose the capital of the company was increased to £700,000 by the creation of that number of shares. This arrangement, by avoiding the purchase of the share capital of Perseverance Mill, effected a considerable saving in stamp duty. The net assets of Perseverance Mill were valued at £319,243. These assets were then sold to C. A. Alston Limited, a wholly owned RFD subsidiary, the name of which was changed to the Perseverance Mill Co Ltd, (the original company of that name having been liquidated on the disposal of its assets to RFD). In the next year's RFD company accounts the sum of £232,459 appeared under the heading of shares premium account and it was explained that this represented the excess of the value of the net assets acquired over the nominal value of the 1,000,000 ordinary shares of two shillings issued as the purchase consideration.

Perseverance Mill, through the Noble family, now became by far the largest shareholders in RFD, and it was natural for Alan Noble, the chairman, to become chairman of RFD in succession to Henry Spencer, who took the opportunity presented by the acquisition to resign from the board. As the managing director of one of the largest steel companies in the country, he had an enormous development programme in front of him which would need his undivided attention. Frank Noble was also invited to join the RFD board, which was completed by Anton van Beugen Bik, who continued as managing director, Philip Lucas, Sir Norman Dixon, Gerald Pritty and John Rawsthorn.

But the Noble family were not happy about the dependence of the company on Anton Bik as managing director—they understandably thought he should have a successor in view. Bik's recommendation for this important position was Alan Wylie, whom he had first met when Wylie was on the staff of Andw W. Barr & Co, the auditors of the Ridgeway Trust. Andw Barr were appointed auditors of the new RFD Company when it was incorporated in 1936 and in due course Wylie was made secretary and accountant of RFD. He left after a few years to join another company of which his father was a director, but not before he had acquired an intimate knowledge of the RFD Company's operations. Wylie readily accepted the invitation to rejoin RFD as joint managing director with Bik, who was made vice-chairman.

In the following year, 1962, Alan Noble had to stand down as chairman of RFD because of ill health and his place was taken by Bik, who continued to be joint managing director with Wylie.

Drastic action to remove the excess capacity of the cotton industry was taken as a result of the passing of the Cotton Industry Act in the same year. The Government allocated £30 million and paid compensation for the 105,000 looms that were scrapped. Perseverance received a grant of 25 per cent towards the cost of installing new automatic plant and associated electronic equipment, leaving a balance of £40,000 (plus a further £12,000) to be paid by the company. Many Lancashire textile companies sold out altogether, and the number of mills in Padiham dropped to three, compared with the seventeen that were operating when Herbert Noble took over 'Old Shah' in 1901. Fortunately for the Perseverance Mill operatives, who shared the anxiety felt throughout Lancashire about the future of the cotton trade, 'Big Albion'—as it was now called—carried on.

111

CHAPTER NINE

FULL CIRCLE

After the logical and sensible link with Perseverance Mill had been forged, RFD allowed themselves to be carried up a blind alley in the fashionable name of diversification. This took the form of the manufacture and marketing of a vending machine called Vendex which was thought to be superior to its competitors because it had the facility of giving change. The board's decision to go ahead with this project was by no means unanimous—Philip Lucas, for one, vigorously opposed it. To its critics it had the defects of being totally unrelated to the company's existing product range; of being outside its manufacturing experience; and of requiring new management and marketing expertise. These objections were over-ridden by a desire to expand the scope of the company's small engineering works.

At the annual general meeting on 21 September 1961 the chairman reported 'It is still not possible to make any reliable appraisal of the likely demand for Vendex' (which did not say much for the homework done before the project was undertaken), adding 'it may be some time before the future of this relatively expensive machine can be foreseen'. That last remark gave the clue to the ultimate weakness of the scheme— Vendex was found to be far more costly to make than had been estimated. This was admitted at the next AGM, when the chairman reported that 'as prospects at the moment seem limited we have, therefore, deemed it provident to write off the remainder of the development expenditure incurred up to date'.

No such mistakes occurred in the next move of RFD to expand its activities. There was everything to be said for the acquisition of Elliott Equipment Limited, RFD's main competitor in the inflatables market. Elliott have already been mentioned in these pages as suppliers of oval liferafts to the Royal Navy—a contract that was something of a sore point with RFD. In the mid-1950s the company, which was owned by P. B. Cow (a subsidiary of the Cory Brothers group) and had moved

The moment of truth. Arthur Harrison, now technical director of GQ Parachutes, being lowered into the rear seat of a modified Meteor 7 in preparation for an early test of the ejection seat developed in conjunction with Folland for the Gnat jet trainer

Although web equipment had been used in the Boer War, it was not standardised by the British Army until 1908, when Mills equipment supplied the pattern shown being demonstrated (*below left*) by a soldier. During the next 50 years (and two world wars) it was developed to the Pattern 1958 equipment illustrated above in marching order; (*below right*) William Lindsey, the American cotton broker, who introduced the Mills-Orndorff woven cartridge belt to Britain and formed the Mills Equipment Company in 1906. The company became part of the RFD Group in 1968

to a factory at Lisburn in Northern Ireland, was not doing too well, so Corys sold the Elliott Equipment part of P.B. Cow to the Lindustries textile and engineering conglomerate, the rest of the company going to Allied Polymer.

After running the business for several years the new owners decided they were not getting enough return on their investment. What better buyer could be found than RFD, who had a factory making a similar product a few miles away at Dunmurry, on the road to Belfast? In 1963 the deal was completed. Some of the Elliott Equipment designs were of little value to RFD, but the oval liferafts were continued after the take-over under the RFD brand name. During the next few years they were gradually phased out and replaced by oval liferafts of RFD design. The most significant development work being done by the company was on inflatable escape slides for aircraft, starting with the Vickers Vanguard turbo-prop airliner and followed by the Vickers VC-10. In order to obtain aircraft acceptance of the engineering work on the chute for the VC-10, Elliott were depending on the help of the Walter Kidde Company, which the reader may remember in connection with automatic inflation heads for liferafts. RFD ultimately took away the engineering design responsibility from Walter Kidde and completed the whole VC-10 project with their own facilities.

The really big event of 1963 was the acquisition of GQ Parachute Company Limited—a company that had the same basic manufacturing function as RFD and was likewise identified with safety and survival. The reader may recall that GQ Parachutes, after being given factory space by Reginald Dagnall at Stoke Road, Guildford, in the early 1930s, had moved to a factory of their own at Woking when RFD was made a public company in 1936. The premises at Woking had previously been used as a roller-skating rink called the Stadium, and in their new role they gradually became known as Stadium Works. With a competitive product and a factory to make it in, all the company needed was an order for parachutes from the Air Ministry to put the business on a sound footing. But this proved to be a long and frustrating business. Meanwhile, the company had to scrape along as best it could with some meagre orders for parachute-carrying bags and wind-direction indicators.

To get the position into perspective it is necessary to go back to 1926, when parachutes were at last officially introduced into the Royal Air Force. (An experimental section had been in operation for a few years but had been closed down.) Unhappily the only fully tested British parachute, Calthrop's Guardian Angel, was obsolete. It had been used during the war to drop secret agents behind the German lines in France, and 500 had been ordered shortly before the Armistice, but it was never taken up by the RAF as standard equipment. In March 1925 Sir Samuel Hoare, the Air Minister, told the House of Commons that he thought the time had come when service aeroplanes ought to be equipped with parachutes, and that he had decided to adopt the American Irvin parachute. He regretted that these parachutes would be American and not British, but he felt that the provision of safety appliances was so urgent that he could not wait any longer for the development of a British model. Later in the year he reported that one-third of the initial order of 2,261 Irvin-type parachutes ordered from the United States would be made in England, after which all future supplies would be manufactured at Letchworth by Irving Air Chute of Great Britain Limited, a newly formed subsidiary of the American parent company. The name of the company was a corruption of Irvin (Leslie Leroy Irvin, the inventor) and was due to a spelling mistake in the articles of association which Irvin allegedly could not afford to have altered.

Irvin had started life as a circus performer—diving into a net from the top of the Big Top was his speciality. Then he turned to making parachute drops from a balloon, for which he was billed as 'Ski-Hi Irvin'. In the First World War he had worked for the Curtis Aeroplane Company and had designed his first parachute, which was an attached type. After the war he joined the famous American parachute test team at McCook Field and in 1919 became the first man in the world to jump with a free-fall parachute (from a DH 4 aeroplane).

The Government had promised Leslie Irvin that if he opened a factory in England they would order parachutes from him—and the Air Ministry officials interpreted this as meaning *only* from him. The agreement was regarded as a running contract for the supply of parachutes whenever they were needed. This granting of a virtual monopoly to Irving Air Chute of Great Britain put the Ministry in an awkward position when GQ Parachutes, a 100 per cent British company, came along a few years later and offered their services as alternative suppliers. They got out of it—for the time being—by sending them this prevaricating letter:

Air Ministry,
London WC2
4th December 1934

Gentlemen,

With reference to your communication of the 19th ultimo, I am directed to inform you that your name has been placed on the list of firms who are eligible to be invited to tender for the supply of parachutes and drogue targets for the services of this Department.

I am, Gentlemen,

Your obedient servant,
(Signed) G. Sudbury
for Director of Contracts

As soon as GQ Parachutes were firmly established in their new premises at Woking in the New Year of 1937 they made a determined effort to get this letter translated into action. At a board meeting in February the policy decision was taken that the company, if requested, would manufacture the Irving parachute. For this contingency they would have an Irving parachute made up ready to submit to the Ministry as a specimen. They would also make up specimens of four types of GQ parachutes and harness and submit them for test immediately. On 10 March a letter was sent to the Ministry offering to help in the production of the 'standard issue of parachute and harness' to the tune of fifty per week (without overtime), adding 'We have ready for your inspection a parachute and harness made to Air Ministry specification.' The Ministry stonewalled, replying that 'the production of parachutes in the numbers required is not presenting any difficulty'.

But this did not satisfy GQ, who reminded the Ministry that it was common practice for the Service Departments, including the Air Ministry, to give contracts to other contractors than the patentees. The Ministry replied that invitations to tender for quantities of parachutes for flares had been sent to the company from time to time, and orders had followed, but 'no invitation to tender for man-carrying parachutes has been sent to you as the source of supply of the approved type is adequate for the Department's requirements'.

GQ returned to the attack on 4 May:

From our standpoint it is much to be regretted that we notice in the last issue of the *Ministry of Labour Gazette* that a further contract has been placed with the Irving Company for parachutes, without going to public tender.

This indicates that a monopoly does exist. We can only repeat that we should have been informed or invited to tender as mentioned in your letter of 4 December 1934. On this point we hope you will be good enough to give us a reply.

We can assure you that given equivalent opportunities, we can supply to the Air Ministry the standard parachute and harness as now supplied by our competitor under similar contract conditions at prices 5 per cent lower than at present quoted, in which circumstances a considerable saving of public money can be effected.

The Ministry acknowledged this letter on 8 May and said 'the matter is under consideration'. This was simply a temporising ploy, of course; they had no intention of inviting GQ Parachutes to tender, and the company made it clear that they knew this in a letter addressed to the Secretary of the Air Council on 23 June:

Again, in this month's *Gazette*, published last week, we note with regret that a further order has been given by the Air Ministry to the American-owned concern of Irving for parachutes: to the British company, GQ Parachute Company, who were informed by the Air Ministry that they were eligible, no application for tender was sent.

We do feel that under the present Air Ministry policy we are not being shown fair treatment, and we must say we are rather concerned that a monopoly should be given to an American company to the exclusion of an all-British parachute concern.

On 5 July the company, in an attempt to force a positive response from the Ministry, sent a telegram addressed to the Secretary, Air Ministry, Adastral House, Kingsway, London:

DIRECTOR OF CONTRACTS. YOUR REFERENCE 365263/34 MAY EIGHTH STOP OUR LETTERS DATED MAY FOURTH, JUNE SECOND AND TWENTY THIRD STOP MAY WE RESPECTFULLY ASK YOUR ATTENTION THESE LETTERS

This telegram did the trick. In their reply eleven days later the Ministry made two significant statements (author's italics):

For the time being the Department is not prepared to order Irving-type parachutes from any other manufacturer than Irving Air Chute of Great Britain, Limited.

I am to add that *a contract is being forwarded to you for parachutes of the GQ type for service trials*, in accordance with your tender dated 6th instant, as amended by your letter RQ/MF of the 8th instant.

These statements added up to the possibility of a break in the apparently permanent and exclusive contract given to Irving Air Chute.

In a letter dated 26 July, GQ claimed that the parachute now being used by the RAF was not a proprietary article because of numerous improvements made to it in conjunction with the Royal Air Force officials at Boscombe Down and elsewhere. Without these improvements, they said, the original Irving parachute was obsolete. Furthermore it used a harness made to patents held by a certain Frederick Spencer Wigley, an employee of the Ministry (who had been helped in the design work by Albert Lethern of the Mills Equipment Company, the makers of the harness, later to become part of the RFD Group). An agreement for the use of the patented inventions by the President of the Air Council had been made. GQ had found out through their own patent agents that no assignments of the patents had been made, but the taxes on them were being paid by the patent agents of Irving Air Chute of Great Britain. As a result, the American parent company of Irving were able to offer for sale to foreign countries parachutes that were largely designed by the Air Ministry, to the detriment of GQ Parachutes' overseas trade. The letter concluded:

> We have endeavoured, during the many months which have intervened since this matter was first initiated, to exercise the greatest forbearance to enable a solution to be found which would be acceptable to everybody. Since then, though sorely tempted on a number of occasions, we have as yet studiously avoided contacting other than Air Ministry Departments, as we felt sure that the justice of our claim could result in our receiving due consideration.
>
> We are now beginning to feel, from your letter of the 16th inst, that an impartial inquiry into all the circumstances is necessary. We therefore make a formal application for an inquiry to be instituted as soon as possible.

In their reply the Ministry confined themselves to saying 'the matter will receive attention'.

On top of the competition they were experiencing from the parent Irvin Company in America, GQ were finding that the mere fact of their exclusion from the Ministry's contracts was preventing them selling their own parachutes to foreign countries. This had become all too clear to Gerald Dean (who joined the GQ board with another of Quilter's friends, James Evans, in 1936) in his efforts to get GQ parachutes accepted in South America. Dean was the sales agent for Fairey Aviation

119

and other aircraft firms in South America. On his advice (and with his financial help) the company sent a sales representative named Turner to give demonstration jumps in various parts of the continent. The tour was a great success from the technical point of view, but no sales were booked because the authorities invariably asked why the GQ parachute was not used by the British Government—to which of course Dean had no effective answer.

Arthur Dickinson was having the same experience in Portugal, where he took a jumper to demonstrate the GQ parachute in direct competition with an Irving representative for an order for a hundred parachutes. Dickinson was rather disturbed to find that his man had to jump from the tail gunner's seat of the Portuguese aeroplane, a procedure he had never experienced before, but all went well and the GQ demonstration was considered to be better than Irving's. Then came the question, 'Why did not the British Government use such an excellent parachute?' The order inevitably went to Irving. Raymond Quilter came up against the same situation in Ireland, where he made the demonstration jumps himself.

Quilter also had an ally in the second of the new directors. As the inventor of the Mae West inflatable life-saving jacket, James Evans knew everyone who mattered in the Air Ministry and he took Quilter round and introduced him in all the right offices. He was also a director of Robinson & Cleaver and a few other fabric companies, and had useful contacts with the Government on that side as well. But GQ Parachutes were still not invited to tender for parachutes.

Then Gerald Dean took up the running. He went to see Wilfrid (later Air Chief Marshal Sir Wilfrid) Freeman, the member of the Air Council for research and development. Freeman, though a Government man, was not in the Air Ministry and was able to go direct to the Minister. He rammed home the point that here was a British company that could not sell competitive parachutes abroad because the Air Ministry had insisted on getting all its requirements from an American-owned company. Faced with this accusation, the Ministry at last admitted that their real reason for not inviting GQ Parachutes to tender was their original undertaking to Leslie Irvin and its interpretation by Ministry officials.

Suddenly in 1938 it all came together. The catalyst was Munich and the near-certainty that war was only just around the corner. All at once the Air Ministry responded to Freeman's intervention and made a complete U-turn in their relations with GQ Parachutes, who overnight became a valuable alternative supplier of parachutes. For their part the company had never lost confidence that they would win through in the end, and were able to meet the demand, when it came, from a new two-storey factory they had recently completed in Portugal Road, Woking. (This was to prove a mistake. 'If we had waited six months,' Dickinson recalls, 'the Government would have built a factory for us. As it was, we built the factory ourselves at a cost of £20,000 and had to pay for it out of the profits we hoped to make.')

After making a tiny profit of £246 in the first year to March 1935, the company had operated at a loss during the struggle for recognition by the Air Ministry. As soon as contracts for parachutes were received, the position rapidly improved. For the year ended 31 March 1939 the net profit was a modest £17,365, and the company paid its first dividend of 10 per cent. During that month parachutes were delivered at the rate of 140 a week. After war broke out in September, on the assurance of increased orders from the Ministry, a further extension of the factory was built in Portugal Road, Woking.

Because he was on the reserve of officers, Raymond Quilter assumed he could immediately rejoin his old regiment when war was declared. To his dismay he was told that his work on parachutes was more important. To make up for being denied the opportunity of active service he approached the War Office with the suggestion that there ought to be someone in every factory who knew the rudiments of bomb-disposal, arguing that the Germans could cause nearly as much disruption by dropping any old load of rubbish on a factory as they could with a delayed action or unexploded bomb. (At the back of his mind he was looking for something with an element of danger so that nobody could accuse him of getting out of the war.) The War Office liked his idea and sent him on the first bomb-disposal course at Melksham. There he met a man named Dixon who was a surveyor in London, and when the air raids started Quilter used to go up to London to work with him on bomb-disposal jobs in the City. Then he went a stage further and started up on his own as an unofficial bomb-disposal unit, tackling unexploded bombs in the gardens of friends round London, often accompanied by his wife. He towed defused bombs from their craters with his cherished Lincoln car. A team at the factory made up tools which he invented himself and which were adopted by the military bomb-disposal crews.

Quilter could not obtain a sufficient petrol allowance to continue running the big Lincoln for business purposes, so he exchanged it for an Alfa Romeo, which satisfied the requirements of the Petroleum Board because it had a smaller engine.

The devastating success of airborne troops in the German invasion of the Low Countries in May 1940 brought home to the British Government their neglect of preparations for this new form of warfare. On 22 June Winston Churchill told his Chief of Staff, 'We ought to have a corps of at least 5,000 parachute troops,' adding, 'advantage must be taken of the summer to train these forces, who can none the less play their part meanwhile as shock troops in home defence.'

A new unit, the Central Landing Establishment, was hurriedly set up at Ringway, Manchester, and training was started using modified Whitley bombers and Irving 28ft parachutes. After a few jumps by the 'pull-off' method, this was abandoned in favour of securing a static line to the ripcord of a free-fall parachute to obtain automatic opening. This system worked fairly satisfactorily but on the 136th jump it failed to function and the parachutist, an RASC driver, was killed. Live jumps were immediately cancelled and on the following day three out of twenty-four parachutes carrying dummies failed to open.

At this point Raymond Quilter was sent for to demonstrate a system for dropping airborne troops that he had submitted to Mr Leslie Hore-Belisha, the War Minister, in 1936. It had been turned down because at that time there was no requirement for airborne troops in the British Army. The idea had been put into Raymond's mind when an uncle who worked in Germany told him he had recently witnessed a mass descent of parachutists which had greatly impressed him. The equipment designed by Quilter and Gregory consisted of the standard 28ft parachute in a redesigned packing system in which the canopy was stowed in a man-carried back pack attached to the aircraft by static line. Its great advantage was that the lines of the parachute were withdrawn ahead of the canopy and were fully extended before the canopy began to fill with air. This ensured that the opening of the parachute was delayed until the parachutist was well clear of the aircraft and there was no sudden jerk when it opened. With the existing free-fall system the canopy was deployed first and the parachutist came to an abrupt halt when the lines were fully deployed.

Using stop watches, cine-cameras and projectors to check the results of countless experimental jumps with dummies, Raymond Quilter

122

spent the next five days putting the finishing touches to the system, spending hours on the telephone to Woking discussing minor modifications that James Gregory produced overnight and rushed up to Ringway by car (for which the Ministry authorised petrol *ad lib*). At the end of that brief, hectic period of development the GQ X-type Statichute system enabled the training of airborne troops to be resumed. It remained in service for the rest of the war—and long afterwards—as the most effective static-line parachute system ever made.

The events at Ringway brought about a change in the strained relations between Irving Air Chute and GQ that was welcomed on both sides. With Irving supplying the parachutes and GQ the Statichute system, Raymond Quilter and Leslie Irvin found themselves working side by side—two experienced parachutists combining to provide the world's finest equipment for the new airborne troops. But it was not all work by any means, and parties in the mess were made memorable by Irvin's famous parlour trick of playing the piano while standing on his head, while Quilter accompanied him on his guitar in the orthodox position. The friendship spread to others in the two companies, GQ's Arthur Dickinson finding a kindred spirit in Irving's Captain Turner, and the two organisations worked closely together.

The GQ factory was laid out and geared for the mass production of parachutes during the war. They were mainly emergency-escape types, but the company also made large numbers of X-type Statichutes for airborne troops and supply-dropping parachutes of various kinds. The load-dropping parachutes grew larger and larger in diameter until a gigantic 96ft prototype was made—it was so big that it had to be packed in the street. However, experiments showed that 64ft diameter was the largest practical size for a single parachute, and a cluster of parachutes was found to be preferable to a single one for heavy drops because it gave greater stability and reduced the risk of damage to the load on landing. The number of parachutes in a cluster varied from three to six—Jeeps and anti-tank guns weighing $1\frac{1}{2}$ tons each were dropped by clusters of three or four 60ft parachutes in the Normandy invasion. By the end of the war a smaller parachute of 42ft diameter with shaped (instead of straight-sided) gores was being used, its advantage being that clusters of them could be dropped at aircraft speeds up to 200mph.

One of the first applications of multi-parachute dropping was the airborne lifeboat designed by Uffa Fox in 1943 (for which RFD supplied the automatic inflation heads of the buoyancy chambers used to right the boat when it splashed down). At first the lifeboat was dropped by a cluster of three 32ft parachutes using the static-line system employed by parachute troops, but this was found to damage the aircraft when the lifeboat was released so a different method had to be devised. It began with a GQ vane-type springloaded pilot parachute being streamed and pulling out a 12ft retarder parachute made of two cloths of different porosities. This opened immediately and controlled the opening behaviour and stability of the main canopies, which were pulled out by the weight of the falling lifeboat. This retarder mechanism was universally used for all heavy supply drops and was made by GQ under Ministry of Aircraft Production contract.

The vane-type pilot parachute, like the Statichute, was patented and was a private venture. The original idea came from James Evans and was developed by Quilter and Gregory. It was the first real improvement in auxiliary parachutes and was taken up by the Americans as well as the British authorities. Another GQ invention, the Parasuit—the first combined parachute, harness, Mae West life-jacket and overall—which had been developed several years before the war, was also delivered to the Royal Air Force.

GQ made the prototypes and large numbers of the type-C container and type-C parachute used for dropping supplies from bomb racks. Ammunition, weapons and stores weighing up to 350lb were dropped in these containers in many battle areas, as well as to partisans behind the enemy lines. Some GQ patents were incorporated in the design of this equipment, and in the mechanism which could delay the parachute opening from one-half to six seconds so that the containers fell below the troops' parachutes in an airborne landing.

GQ Parachutes did not have any satellite factories during the war but many other firms—among them Courtaulds and Littlewoods—made parachutes to GQ specifications. Although GQ had an overall watching brief, the contractors worked independently, with their own AID inspectors, who used to come down to Woking to sort out any manufacturing problems that had arisen. As in the case of RFD, the supplies of fabric were controlled by the Ministry. Silk was in short supply at the beginning of the war so it was reserved for escape parachutes until nylon fabrics became available. In fact nylon was better than silk because it was more resistant to mildew and the attacks of sundry insects. Parachutes for airborne troops and supply dropping were usually made of lightweight cotton and rayon, care having to be taken to keep them aired to avoid deterioration caused by damp.

Packing parachutes has always been a (literally) vital operation, and during the war it was done with infinite care and the utmost reliability by members of the Women's Auxiliary Air Force. It took about 25min to fold, stow and inspect each parachute, which was unpacked and repacked every two months to avoid the dangers of creasing and damp. Parachute life was restricted to twenty-five descents.

Raymond Quilter was chairman of the Parachute Panel and of the Airborne Forces Committee during the war. When it was all over he received an *ex gratia* award of £27,500 'in full and final settlement of your claim for past, present and future use by the Crown of your inventions and designs, and for the exceptional services rendered by you to the Crown'. This was of course free of tax. The company itself received a cheque for £5,520 (after deduction of £2,250 income tax) for present and future user of inventions which were subject to certain patents. Both these cheques came from the Ministry of Supply, not from the Commission of Awards to Inventors, to whom no applications were made.

Unlike many companies, GQ Parachutes did not benefit financially from the war. As Arthur Dickinson explained:

When the excess profits tax came in at the beginning of the war, we hadn't got a pre-war standard of profits to work on—we had run at a loss in 1937 and 1938 and only made a small profit in 1939. The result was that although the profit and turnover went up many times during the war, in fact all the profit, and more, went in paying EPT. So we emerged from the war rather worse off than we had been at the beginning. We owed a large amount of EPT, but we were able to set off against that the repayment of a certain percentage of EPT that had already been paid, and that helped our financial position.

At the end of the war about 500 people were employed at Woking, but the payroll had to be cut back to 70 to 80 while fresh work was found to replace the cancelled contracts for military material. Like RFD, GQ Parachutes found a respite in making clothing, and during the next two or three years the output of women's skirts went up to about 2,000 a week. From 1947 onwards the Government started to order parachutes again and with the outbreak of the Korean war in 1950 there was such a demand for parachutes—particularly for Canberra aircrews —that the company closed down the clothing department.

At this stage the Government decided to restrict parachute contracts to two suppliers, Irving Air Chute for man-dropping parachutes and GQ for supply dropping and other parachute uses—a distinction that very soon became blurred. At the same time it was now Government policy to transfer design approval for items of equipment from the various research establishments to industry. As a result of this decision both the parachute companies gained design approval and in 1953 GQ opened a separate drawing office and design department.

In the previous year, on 18 September 1952, the company lost a true friend in the death of Sir Cuthbert Quilter Bt, Raymond's father, at the age of seventy-nine. His initial, albeit guarded financial support had been followed by guarantees of bank overdrafts backed by securities, and in 1939 he was appointed a director 'to supervise the increased financial operations of the company' resulting from Air Ministry contracts. After the war he had provided a considerable sum of money by the creation of a 5 per cent mortgage debenture, which was redeemed some years after his death. Raymond now became Sir Raymond Quilter, 3rd baronet.

The 1950s saw a tremendous surge of development and production by GQ Parachutes, partly on a private-venture basis, partly in conjunction with the Royal Aircraft Establishment and partly on direct Ministry contracts. In many cases GQ patents were involved.

An important new use for parachutes was found in the initial braking of aircraft on landing. Since the war aircraft had grown heavier and faster, with the consequence that their landing speeds had increased. Runways had been lengthened accordingly, but there was a limit to which this could be done. Reversible-pitch propellers for propeller-driven aircraft and reversible thrust on jet aircraft were developed to reduce the length of the landing run, and further assistance was given by the brake parachute, which had the merit that it exerted its maximum braking force at the start of the landing run when the speed was highest and the wheel brakes were likely to be least effective. GQ played a leading part in developing and supplying the brake parachute by buying the 24-litre Napier-Railton car with which John Cobb had set up the outright lap record of 143mph at Brooklands before the war, and using it as a test vehicle. Raymond Quilter enjoyed himself hugely driving the car in the test sessions at Dunsfold aerodrome, accelerating along the runway before releasing the parachute carried in a housing mounted on the tail, from which it was extracted by a spring-loaded vane-type parachute. The brake parachute was retracted into the housing before the end of the runs. GQ supplied brake parachutes for various aircraft ranging in size from 7ft 6in for the Folland Gnat to 45ft for the Victor V-bomber.

Another new use discovered for parachutes was in preventing prototype aircraft getting into an uncontrollable spin while undergoing stalling and spinning tests. GQ made them under sub-contract for many aircraft including the DH-110, the Hunter, the Gnat, the Javelin and the Victor V-bomber.

The three V-bombers were originally designed to have rocket-assisted take-off units in the form of de Havilland Sprite and Spectre liquid-fuelled rocket motors carried in pods, two to each aircraft. The pods were jettisoned after take-off and had a parachute recovery system designed and developed by GQ Parachutes.

Ministry of Supply contracts were also received for parachutes to recover missile test vehicles and meteorological research sounding rockets from extremely high altitudes and speeds.

The parachute itself was developed in a variety of ways. In 1955 a 66ft segmented canopy was made for dropping heavy loads of up to 4,500lb and a cluster of eight of these parachutes was able to handle a load of 30,000lb. At the other end of the scale a utility parachute for dropping a 500lb load at 130 knots was produced at less than half the cost of the one it superseded, and a high-velocity utility parachute was developed for dropping one-ton loads at high landing speeds. The thinnest parachute pack made so far, designed for roving crew members of the RAF, was matched by a similar one for use in helicopters. The existing 42ft parachute was modified, and lightweight low-bulk canopies of $18\frac{1}{2}$ and 20ft diameter were introduced. Then there was a torpedo parachute, a sonobuoy parachute for stabilising radio marker buoys, and a parachute for extracting heavy loads from aircraft and deploying the main parachute. A stabilising parachute for controlling human fall from high altitudes was developed, and a flexible-back automatic escape-type parachute which was used in Germany and Holland.

To cope with the increased output of parachutes a new factory of two single-storey buildings with a total area of 20,000sq ft was built in 1956 at Knaphill, about three miles outside Woking, at a cost of £50,000. It formed an extension of the main production workshop at Woking with long tables for packing large brake and supply-dropping parachutes. An air-flow test rig was installed for checking out air-ventilated suits.

A great deal of development work was also done on parachute harness, and this resulted in the production of the Z-type safety harness, which became standard in most British and many foreign aircraft; a combined cord harness and overall which was loose fitting, self-adjusting and very comfortable; a special harness for strapping people to stretchers; and an air–sea rescue harness for use with helicopters.

In 1949 GQ Parachutes tackled the problem of providing a parachute that would open automatically at a pre-determined height of say 10,000ft regardless of the altitude at which it had been released. Experiments had shown that a parachute released at a great height opened so suddenly (for atmospheric reasons) that the shock could injure the parachutist and damage his parachute. It might also cause him to lose his oxygen mask, with fatal results on a long descent from a high altitude. A device was therefore required to enable the parachutist to drop to a safe height before his parachute automatically opened. GQ supplied a prototype comprising a barometric device which operated an explosive charge at a fixed height and pulled the ripcord. Irving worked on a similar device incorporating a compressed coil spring.

Both these solutions assumed that the pilot would be able to get out of a turbo-jet aircraft flying fast and high, but in reality this was not possible. Accordingly, although the automatic opening device was used in Britain, Canada, Sweden and Germany for parachute drops at lower altitudes and speeds, work proceeded on the development of an ejection seat which would carry the pilot well clear of the aircraft. The Swedish Saab Company claimed to have used an ejection seat propelled by an explosive charge for the first time in 1943, three years ahead of Martin-Baker, whose ejection seat was demonstrated 'live' by Bernard Lynch on 24 July 1946, flying in a Meteor at a height of 8,000ft and a speed of 320mph.

In 1954 the British Government ordered a small jet trainer, the Folland Gnat, based on the Midge light fighter, which was too small to accommodate the standard Martin-Baker seat now being used with an Irving parachute in the Meteor and other service aircraft. Not wishing to put all the ejection-seat business in the hands of these two suppliers, the Government asked Folland to make a new lightweight ejection seat for the Gnat and commissioned GQ Parachutes to design a complete parachute assembly for it. As the two companies would be working closely together, Sir Raymond Quilter was given a seat on the board of Folland Aviation.

The assembly comprised the mechanism for releasing the pilot from his seat immediately after he left the aircraft, a small drogue to bring him into a standing position and reduce his initial speed, and a stabilising parachute to reduce his speed still further and lessen the tendency for him to spin while he came down to a pre-determined height at which the main parachute was opened automatically by a barometrically operated capsule.

T. W. (Dumbo) Willans, who had been awarded the Royal Aeronautical Society's silver medal for his parachute work, had offered to be the guinea-pig for the Folland ejection seat when the Gnat was first mooted, and he was now taken on to further the project, together with Arthur Harrison, one of the few professional free-fall delayed-drop parachutists in the country.

In the spring of 1954 Raymond Quilter had decided to sponsor the British team for the second world parachuting championships to be held in France in August, a gesture that cost the company about £5,000. He asked Harrison, who lived near the works at Woking, to select and train the six-man team. Harrison picked his men from the RAF parachute training school at Weston-on-the-Green in Oxfordshire, and in six weeks had brought them up to a reasonable standard. Quilter provided his own Dragon Rapide aircraft, which he flew himself, for the practice drops at Weston-on-the-Green, and of course the company provided the parachutes. Those used in the championships were later donated by Quilter to the British Parachute Club when it was formed at Denham in November 1955.

Although the British team were unplaced in the championships, they left their mark by introducing an advance in technique—the blank gore parachute—which greatly improved manoeuvrability. This was copied by the Russians in the next world championships and was subsequently used by most countries taking part in sport parachuting.

When it was all over, Harrison accepted Quilter's invitation to join the company and gave up his job at the Government operational research establishment at Byfleet to become project engineer at GQ. In that capacity he was packed off to Canada in the new year of 1956 to sort out the parachute problems arising from the modernisation of the Royal Canadian Air Force. Quilter told him he would only be away for three or four weeks, but the job actually took twenty-one months to complete.

It was in 1956 that Raymond Quilter indulged another of his exuberant whims when he took to flying his personal standard on the roof of the Dorchester Hotel in London when he was in residence in his permanent suite. That this custom was normally reserved for visiting monarchs and statesmen staying at the hotel did not worry him in the least. 'I'm a simple sort of person really,' he explained to a newspaper reporter, 'I believe in the old things of England—chivalry and all that sort of thing. In the old days those with flags used to fly them. I think this custom should be carried on. Mine's not a bad flag — it's properly made to scale, and I'm proud of it.'

For Sir Raymond Quilter the family motto, 'Rather die than change', was not to be lightly dismissed. The standard bore the Quilter arms: *Arg. on a bend invected gu. between three Cornish Choughs bendwise, ppr. two cross-crosslets of the field.*

The first live test of the Folland–GQ ejection seat was made by Dumbo Willans on 21 December 1956 in a modified Meteor 7 piloted by Dick Whittington, a Folland test pilot, after taking off from Chilbolton airfield near Andover. In his book, *Parachuting and Sky-diving*, Willans described what happened.:

> At 5,000ft over Salisbury Plain at an air speed of 150 knots and wind speed at ground of 15 knots, I received my 5-second countdown from Dick and ejected above cloud. As I yanked the canvas blind down over my face, an enormous acceleration threw me into the slipstream and the parachute opened automatically. The seat fell free and was picked up almost undamaged.
>
> I waved to Ted Tennant, Folland's chief test pilot, who passed me in a Proctor aircraft, and landed safely after a very stable descent.

When Arthur Harrison returned from Canada, he lost no time in taking his share of the development of the Folland–GQ ejection seat and clocked up five test drops from the Meteor 7. (The system was to stay in production until 1978, when the Gnat was replaced by the Hawker Siddeley Hawk, which was fitted with a Martin-Baker ejection seat and a GQ parachute.)

The success of the Folland Gnat ejection seat resulted in the Swedish Air Force, which had a rather poor record with its own parachute system, asking GQ to re-design the ejection-seat system for the new Saab J.35 Draken (Dragon). It was a rush job which had to be completed in three months, and the equipment passed its test with flying colours

Protection from the splash of molten steel at approximately 1600°C is given to blast furnacemen and hot metal operators by the 'Furnaceman' clothing made by RFD Mills Equipment. The woollen fabric is soft and pliable and allows comfortable freedom of movement in the heaviest work

A cluster of seven 66ft cargo parachutes dropping a heavy military load. Eight of these GQ parachutes were used for the greatest load ever dropped by parachute – 40,000lb (17.85 tons) of steel plates dropped from a Blackburn Beverley aircraft over Brough, Yorkshire, in 1962 (*vide The Guinness Book of Records*, 1965)

exactly three months to the day after the specification was written. The GQ system was later used for the Saab J.37 Viggen (Forked Lightning).

Meanwhile, the period of enthusiasm and development in the 1950s had come to a sudden and sombre end when Sir Raymond Quilter Bt, the very mainspring of the company, died on 7 February 1959 at the early age of fifty-seven. Many tributes were paid to him for his fine qualities and achievements, but none more expressive than that in the *Sunday Times* under the heading 'What a Life!' written by his old friend Henry Longhurst:

> If a boy delights in lying on his back between the rails at night for the pleasure of watching express trains run over him and can later claim to have been birched more times in a given period than any other Etonian, it may be taken as likely that he will grow up to be something of a 'character'. This was certainly true of Sir Raymond Quilter, and the world is much, much the poorer for his loss.
>
> Versatile and eccentric, inventive yet extremely practical, he must have packed a greater variety of experience into his 56 years than most men would contrive if they had their lives six times over.
>
> I met him first in connection with golf, which was in a sense the only one of his abiding interests which ever defeated him. He attacked it with tremendous vigour and saw no reason why, with a few intelligent modifications here and there, it should not, like anything else, be made to work. He easily got down to scratch, of course, but despite a succession of short cuts, hints, tips, new sets of clubs and hundreds of hours of practice, the ultimate secret evaded him. It was almost the only one that did . . .
>
> He was one of the three people whom I would class as the best company I have ever known. No one can have brought a more instant enlivenment to the party by his arrival or reduced more people to actual tears of laughter. In its way it is a tribute to the humble game of golf to have been the only thing that beat him.

But he had another, serious, side. Talking about him one day to Lady Quilter during the war, Professor Reginald Gibbs, who was in charge of the scientific aspect of parachutes at Farnborough, remarked: 'You know, Raymond is a most astonishing person. He has absolutely no education as we understand it, but he's got a mind like blotting paper. He forgets nothing you tell him, and altogether he's got a quite remarkable brain.'

From all accounts Raymond Quilter had a degree of personal magnetism that made everybody want to do things for him, with the result that he surrounded himself with a most devoted collection of people.

At the next board meeting Arthur Dickinson took Raymond Quilter's place as managing director and Edward Baldrey OBE, the senior partner in the firm of accountants who had been the auditors for the past nineteen years, was elected chairman. At the following meeting James Gregory, one of the two founders, at last joined the board and was appointed chief designer, a position he had held *de facto* since the company was formed. At the same time the board was greatly strengthened by the addition of Air Marshal Sir Gordon Harvey, KBE, CB, who had joined the company two years earlier as controller of research and development. Sir Gordon commanded the Airborne Forces Experimental Establishment in 1940 and had been Air Officer C-in-C, Maintenance Command RAF before he retired from the service in 1956.

For the rest of the year Dickinson worked on a reorganisation plan which involved getting rid of two small subsidiary companies, GQ Aircraft Developments and Technical Cinematographic Requirements, which were losing money, and some items of equipment—the Dragon Rapide aircraft kept at Fair Oaks, the Napier–Railton car used for the development (now completed) of the brake parachute, and the big Ford Fairlane saloon which had replaced the Lincoln used by Raymond Quilter before the war—which were no longer required.

On the positive side an industrial division was formed under James Gregory to exploit the commercial possibilities of the company's experience. One of the first products was a combined safety harness and protective suit which was supplied mainly to the Coal Board. This was followed by a general-purpose safety harness that was suitable for people working at dangerous heights and in conditions above or below ground where some form of suspension or restraint was needed. Unhappily James Gregory was given only a few years to develop the division. He died on 24 March 1962, leaving behind a legacy of parachute design and development which was one of the company's greatest assets.

Arthur Dickinson decided that if he was going to run the company his way there would have to be a radical change in the management style. Raymond Quilter had dominated the organisation with its 300 men and women as a benevolent autocrat, but this was obviously not his style. Instead, he appointed people to be individually responsible for various functions—production, accounts, buying and selling—under his overall control as managing director. After a time he succeeded in building up a good team who worked on the basis of mutual trust.

Then he thought about the future. Being a private company had been of considerable personal benefit to Raymond Quilter, but now he had gone the disadvantages became apparent. They would be better off within a larger organisation, but he was in no hurry—he certainly wasn't going to hawk the company around. He thought they would have some offers, possibly from one of the aircraft companies—Blackburn, for example—with whom they had worked closely, but nothing happened. Then Anton Bik of RFD asked him to lunch:

> He told me that RFD had been asked to take over a small private company called Airborne Industries who made parachutes and air–sea rescue equipment at Leigh-on-Sea. Bik pointed out that this would mean RFD getting into the parachute business—something that Reginald Dagnall had voluntarily promised Raymond Quilter he would never do when they had to part company in 1936. A much better plan, Bik suggested, would be for GQ to join RFD. In that way the wheel would turn full circle.

The GQ board welcomed the idea—the two companies were in many respects complementary and had always been in close touch. On RFD's side the proposal was attractive because the large amounts of textiles used by GQ would benefit Perseverance Mill, who had joined RFD later in the year of Quilter's death. And there was the added prospect of RFD's engineering works being able to supply metal components for GQ parachute harness.

The terms of the RFD offer to acquire all the issued capital of GQ were agreed by the RFD shareholders at an extraordinary general meeting held at Grosvenor House on 9 October 1964. The net assets of GQ were valued at £329,806, represented by share capital of £115,000, revenue reserves of £70,000 and unappropriated surplus of £144,806 on profit and loss account. There would be a cash consideration of £70,000 and the balance would be met by the allotment and issue of 800,000 RFD ordinary shares of two shillings each credited as fully paid up. The difference between the net value of the GQ assets and the consideration paid for them resulted in an increase of £241,643 in the RFD share premium account. In the last full year before the acquisition GQ made a profit before taxation of £93,184, more than double the figure of £44,846 in 1954.

With two major manufacturing subsidiaries, Perseverance Mill and GQ Parachutes, added to the original RFD Company, the time was opportune to restructure the business on a more rational basis. This was agreed at the meeting on 9 October and was done by separating the manufacturing and trading activities (inflatables) of the RFD company from its functions as a share-holding and property-owning company. The manufacturing and trading side became a subsidiary retaining the original name while the holding company became the RFD Group. To provide the ordinary shares needed for the GQ acquisition and to provide for future expansion, the capital of the RFD Group was increased by £300,000 to £1 million.

Anton Bik and Alan Wylie, the joint managing directors of the RFD Group, joined the board of GQ Parachute Company and Arthur Dickinson, as managing director of the GQ subsidiary, was given a place on the RFD Group board.

CHAPTER TEN

'TO WEAR WEAPONS AND SERVE IN THE WARS'*

Another six years were to pass before the RFD Group made its next acquisition. In the meantime there was work to be done in helping the semi-autonomous companies meet their changing market conditions.

Perseverance Mill, for example, where much of the machinery was old-fashioned and out-of-date, were assisted in 1962-3 to the tune of £52,000 in buying high-speed automatic plant and associated electronic equipment to meet the accelerating shift towards the use of synthetic fabrics. A quarter of the cost of the new plant was met initially by a Government cotton trade re-equipment grant. The severe recession in the Lancashire cotton trade in the mid-1960s caused by the high level of imports necessitated a further reduction in the number of cotton looms. These were replaced by modern high-speed equipment suitable for weaving synthetic fabrics, but some disruption occurred while it was being installed. Turnover went up during the late 1960s, but profits were lower.

As we have seen, Perseverance had been making cotton typewriter ribbon since the early 1920s. After the Second World War nylon yarn became available for weaving, but its use for typewriter ribbon presented difficulties because nylon, unlike cotton, does not absorb ink. To obtain satisfactory ink retention it was found necessary to use not only more filaments (34 instead of the usual 14) in the thread, but also filaments of smaller diameter and weight. This enabled ink to be retained through the interstices of the weave and between the filaments which make up a single thread.

This fine-filament thread became available for the first time in the United States in the early 1960s. Jeremy Higham saw its potentialities and imported supplies to start weaving experiments while trying to persuade Imperial Chemical Industries to produce it for the British market. He also had to convince the typewriter-ribbon trade that nylon

* Articles of Religion: Of the Civil Magistrates.

was superior to cotton. He succeeded in both endeavours, and Perseverance switched to ICI for their supplies of 34-filament nylon thread for making typewriter and computer ribbons.

In 1967 Jeremy Higham spent a fortnight in the United States and took the opportunity to call on some old friends of the company who marketed both nylon and cotton typewriter ribbons. They mentioned the company that slit their wide reels of fabric into narrow widths, and took Jeremy along to meet them. He found that the machine the company had developed was unique in the accuracy with which it produced narrow-width ribbons with perfect edges. To his surprise they asked him whether he would like to have one on a royalty basis—a percentage on the gross price of the product. This offer had momentous consequences, as Jeremy Higham recalls:

> We got one of the machines over here and it enabled us to gain a foothold in the market before anyone else. What is more, we got the world rights for it outside the United States. Nobody else can have a machine like this, and it's put us in a tremendously strong position.

It was not long before a second machine was installed.

In the period immediately after they were taken over, GQ Parachutes were actually making more money than the parent company. Indeed, the prospects were so bright that the Group board readily agreed to finance a new factory at Waterlooville in Hampshire in 1965. This proved to be a mistake because three years later Government defence economies cut back the parachute contracts on which the Woking and Knaphill factories largely depended. They had to be kept going at all costs, so Waterlooville was starved of work.

At that moment a rumour reached Alan Wylie, the managing director of the RFD Group, that the Mills Equipment Company Limited, an old-established private company from whom both RFD and GQ purchased webbing for parachute harness and other safety equipment, would not be unwilling to be taken over. Wylie immediately got in touch with Gerald Fairlie, a Mills executive director, and together they worked out a scheme to the satisfaction of both parties. For the RFD Group the acquisition of Mills Equipment would fulfil the main conditions of a successful take-over. As manufacturers of textile-based products—they were the pioneer producers of military webbing equipment—the company were in the same line of business as RFD, and there would be no need to find new management to run it. Above all, the acquisition of Mills Equipment would provide work for the under-utilised GQ factory at Waterlooville.

On the other side, being taken over would solve long-term difficulties that had been building up at Mills Equipment for some years. But before coming to those problems let us trace the history of that company from the beginning.

The Mills story really began on 27 August 1867 when Captain Anson Mills of the 18th Infantry, United States Army, took out a patent covering the manufacture of a cartridge belt made of leather, canvas or webbing with a series of light cylindrical receptacles or loops for carrying cartridges. He reckoned that this would be lighter than the usual cartridge boxes and the weight would be better distributed on the wearer. Unhappily two snags emerged when the idea was put into practice. It was difficult to make the cartridge loops uniform in size, and the stitching attaching the loops to the belt deteriorated too quickly. Mills decided that these difficulties could be overcome by using a webbing belt with the loops woven integrally with the backing of the belt, but that was easier said than done. In fact it was an exceedingly tricky problem for an expert weaver—let alone a mere soldier—and it took Mills ten years of experimenting with various loom attachments before patenting the Mills cartridge-belt loom on 9 July 1877.

The first complete loom was perfected and built by Crompton & Knowles at Worcester, Massachusetts, in 1880 under a further Mills patent. The woven cartridge belt with built-in loops was first manufactured by Charles W. Gilbert in the same town in 1880, and was adopted in the same year by the United States Army as the regulation cartridge belt. Two years later manufacture was taken over by Thomas C. Orndorff, a brother-in-law of Anson Mills, and the Anson Mills–Orndorff Cartridge Belt Company was formed.

The belt with a single row of cartridges was followed by one with a double row holding 100 cartridges, which in turn was adopted by the US Army and led to the Anson–Orndorff factory being considerably enlarged. The next step was to make a belt with pockets that would take the clips of cartridges used in the Lee machine gun, the forerunner of the Lee–Enfield rifle. To weave pockets, instead of loops, integrally with the belt presented more technical problems, but these were overcome in patents taken out in 1889. (A satisfactory cartridge belt with pockets for clips was not however produced until 1900.) While this was going on, Anson Mills, who had a flair for inventing, patented a new type of belt fastener with a C-shaped brass hook and two brass slides which was to become a standard fitting.

Anson Mills–Orndorff got most of their cotton yarn from a Boston, Mass, broker named William Lindsey, and they in turn were his largest customer. Lindsey became deeply interested in the production of cartridge belts, and when the Boer War broke out in 1899 he felt there would be a reasonable chance of doing good business with the British Government. After some intensive negotiations with Anson Mills (by now General Anson Mills, US Army, retired) Lindsey bought the rights to manufacture belts in Great Britain and immediately made arrangements to ship a few looms to England. He then sailed across the Atlantic himself, taking with him Edward B. Allen as factory manager. On arrival he rented some premises known as Alpine and Bolton Works at Stoke Newington in North-East London and sent for two American mechanics to come over and install the machinery. He also set up the Mills Woven Cartridge Belt Company in an office at 32 Victoria Street, Westminster.

Only then did Lindsey ask for an interview with the Quartermaster-General of the British Army, Lieutenent-General Sir Henry Brackenbury, to whom he showed sample belts which fortunately suited the British cartridge, since this was of the same diameter as the American. Sir Henry had no hesitation in approving the woven cartridge belt in principle but pointed out that the Army's need for equipment was so urgent that they could not wait for the belts to be shipped from America. William Lindsey calmly explained that this would present no difficulty because he had a factory in England which could start work at a moment's notice. His confidence in setting up a plant before he had got any orders astounded the general, and he placed an order for thousands of belts on the spot.

Further orders followed as the war went on and it soon became apparent that the little factory at Stoke Newington could not produce enough belts, even with the additional looms Lindsey had obtained from America. The demand for hundreds of thousands of cartridge belts was eventually met with the help of shipments from the Anson Mills–Orndorff factory at Worcester, Mass. Until the end of the Boer War in 1902 the British and American factories were running at full production to meet War Office requirements for cartridge belts, bando-

A single 66ft parachute carrying a load of 4,500lb

The RFD PB-16 Z-boats used by the trans-British Columbia expedition led by Captain Sir Ranulph Twistleton-Wikeham-Fiennes in 1971 traversed hundreds of rapids, including some that had never before been successfully navigated. The expedition was accompanied by a two-man BBC television crew and the *Observer*'s top photographer

Three of the six RFD passenger escape slides carried by the Concorde are quickly convertible into sea survival rafts with canopies. A separate 36-seater liferaft is also carried. The airworthiness regulations stipulate that the full complement of passengers must be able to leave the aircraft within 90 seconds of the warning to evacuate being given, when all passengers and cabin attendants are seated with safety belts fastened. In an exercise carried out in darkness with emergency lighting only inside the aircraft, the evacuation was completed in 86 seconds

(*left*) The captive balloon, originally made for artillery observation in World War I by Reginald Dagnall at Airships Limited and by RFD as the barrage balloon in World War II, is nowadays supplied to the Army for training parachutists

(*right*) Linesmen maintaining overhead electricity cables can work in safety with the help of the pole-belt supplied by RFD Mills Equipment

liers, rifle slings and water-bottle slings. Bandoliers were produced because it was discovered that the British troops, instead of wearing the cartridge belts as belts, actually wore them as bandoliers across the chest. Mills and Orndorff accordingly designed a double-loop and pocket bandolier with a triangular fastening to carry a bayonet frog, which was covered by a British patent.

In addition, in response to the need for every soldier in South Africa to carry extra ammunition into battle, a very light and flimsy bandolier was produced, solely for use in battle, which could be thrown away afterwards. These bandoliers, woven to accommodate 100 cartridges in loops, were filled before being packed for transportation so that they would be ready for immediate issue to the troops in the field. The idea was excellent in theory, but owing to the difficulties in equipping the mounted infantry, the men were forced to use the emergency bandoliers as part of their regular equipment. The result was disastrous. The light texture of the bandoliers could not stand up to campaign conditions for any length of time (nor was it intended to); consequently the woven loops stretched and would not hold the cartridges firmly. The mounted infantry lost many thousands of rounds of ammunition in this way.

After the war this unfortunate experience with the emergency bandolier was seized upon to condemn the use of webbing equipment as a whole. In spite of the initial approval of the Quartermaster-General, it had been accepted grudgingly by many people in the Army, who could not envisage anything being better than leather. In the reports on the war issued afterwards by Lord Kitchener, Lord Roberts, General French, General Plumer and General Baden-Powell, webbing equipment was universally condemned—always on account of the poor performance of the misused emergency bandolier.

The authorities thereupon rejected webbing equipment and reverted to leather as the material for the Pattern 1903 Bandolier Equipment which comprised belt, ammunition pouches, bandolier, and separate straps for haversack, water-bottle and fastening the greatcoat. This equipment was adopted for the British Army and eventually all Imperial and Colonial troops.

William Lindsey was so discouraged by this turn of events that he went back to the United States, leaving a skeleton staff in Victoria Street under William Pierrepoint Wise, a young American of outstanding enterprise and ambition, in the hope that he might be able to re-open negotiations with the British authorities. Wise began by approaching Captain John Jellicoe, Director of Ordnance at the Admiralty (later to become Admiral of the Fleet Earl Jellicoe), whom he had met in the Far East in 1900 on an abortive trip to sell cartridge belts to the Japanese. He had found they were using a rifle clip similar to that in the German Mauser, so the belt with loops for single cartridges did not interest them. Wise thereupon made a sketch of a belt with woven pockets for clips and sent it to General Mills in Worcester, who succeeded in producing a satisfactory specimen. The twenty belts shipped to Japan for trials were the first woven pocket belts made, and they enabled the company to keep pace with the change from single cartridges to rifle clips. The Japanese then insisted on the equipment being made locally, which Lindsey thought was too risky, so Wise went on to China. There he made the acquaintance of Captain Jellicoe, who was chief of staff to Admiral Sir E. H. Seymour and had commanded the international contingents sent ashore to protect the various legations during the Boxer rebellion.

Now, five years later, Captain Jellicoe remembered being shown the webbing belt by Wise in China. He authorised Captain Percy Scott to have some unofficial trials carried out at Whale Island, Portsmouth, using Navy pattern webbing equipment which Wise had designed in collaboration with some favourably inclined officers at the training establishment.

Wise's attempts to get in touch with the War Office were not so successful. Then a curious chain of events led to his meeting General Baden-Powell, Inspector of Cavalry, and one of the fiercest critics of webbing equipment (as represented by the wretched emergency bandolier) in the Boer War. Briefly, this occurred because Wise decided to call on Jacques Lebaud, a sugar king who had arrived in London with the crazy idea of forming an 'Empire in the Sahara'. At the Savoy Hotel Wise was referred to Lebaud's chief-of-staff, Colonel Gourand. He gave Wise a letter of introduction to General Baden-Powell.

Wise seized the opportunity to re-open the question of webbing belts and showed the general some specimen belts with woven pockets for rifle clips, each pocket being fitted with a separate flap to prevent loss of ammunition. Baden-Powell was sufficiently impressed to authorise unofficial trials to be held at Aldershot by General Scobell, commanding the cavalry.

Reports on both the Portsmouth and Aldershot unofficial trials were favourable, and in the autumn of 1905 Major-General Herbert Plumer, Quartermaster-General of the Army Council, at the behest of Baden-Powell, called a meeting at the War Office at which General Mulcahy, the Director of Equipment and Stores, and Colonel Wrigley (both of whom were webbing-equipment enthusiasts) were present. At the end of the discussion General Plumer was persuaded to agree to a short official trial being carried out at Aldershot with forty sets of the Navy pattern equipment.

In the meantime negotiations with foreign Governments met with a certain amount of success—as well as some rebuffs. Orders from the Italian Navy Department were received in 1903, and later from the Norwegian and Dutch navies. This meant work for the Mills factory and was a useful stop-gap. There also seemed a prospect of doing business with the German and French Governments, and arrangements were made to set up small plants in Paris and Berlin to weave cartridge carriers and make up military webbing equipment. Every effort was made to induce the French authorities to adopt webbing equipment, and designs to meet their particular needs were produced and demonstrated. It was all to no avail, of course, because the inevitable French chauvinism effectively blocked the way. Much the same thing happened in Berlin and both plants were shipped back to London. These ventures cost a lot of money and it was not unreasonable for William Lindsey to keep writing from the States threatening to close the whole business down.

In 1906 the tide in favour of webbing equipment took a positive turn. It started in June when Major R. Burrowes of the 87th Royal Irish Fusiliers went along to the War Office with his patented idea for re-designing the infantryman's equipment to improve the weight distribution between front and back. Although his specification described the equipment as being made of leather, the War Office told him to go to the Mills Woven Cartridge Belt Company to discuss the question of manufacturing it in webbing. (Major Burrowes' visit to the company's offices in Victoria Street, on which the fortunes of the Mills company were to turn, made a lifelong impression on a newly joined junior member of the staff named Albert Lethern, who forty years later became managing director.)

Fundamentally the Mills–Burrowes web equipment was composed of two parts. The first enabled the soldier to carry on his belt his bayonet, ammunition, waterbottle and haversack. Together with his rifle (carried on a sling), this was called 'marching order without pack'. The second part of the equipment comprised the pack and supporting straps, which did not cross his chest and therefore did not restrict his breathing. The soldier could instantly discard this bulkier portion of his kit without sacrificing his fighting efficiency.

Perhaps the most important feature was that all the components were connected together so that the whole equipment could be put on and taken off in one motion. This had two advantages: a soldier could turn out of barracks or camp fully equipped in a few moments, even in the dark, and on the march he could slip off his equipment when a halt was called and put it on again quickly when the order was given to fall in. And of course the clever balance of the equipment—once it was properly fitted—meant that it did not ride on the shoulders, regardless of whether the front ammunition pouches or the back pack were full or empty. Given that the soldier had to carry a heavy load, the Mills–Burrowes equipment was the most comfortable and least tiring method of doing so.

Burrowes was more interested in the design of his equipment than in the material it was made of, and he quickly established a good relationship with the company. The next step was to prepare manufacturing specifications, in which considerable help was received from Francis Stevenson & Sons Limited of Dundee in the matter of khaki dyeing and moisture-proofing of the high-quality cotton yarn—an association that was to continue for many years.

When this news reached William Lindsey in America he realised that the equipment would have a very much better chance of being accepted if the firm responsible for the final design and manufacture were an English one instead of being a business controlled by an individual American. He came over to London in August 1906 and formed a British company, the Mills Equipment Company Limited, with £10,000 capital subscribed by English shareholders including Lord Davey and his son, the Honourable Arthur J. Davey. It started to operate on 1 October 1906. Mr Davey was appointed chairman and William P. Wise the managing director. The other directors were a barrister and a stockbroker.

Close collaboration between Major Burrowes and the company resulted in a satisfactory arrangement whereby the company agreed to pay a royalty to Burrowes during the life of a new patent applied for in the joint names of the Mills Equipment Company Limited and the Hon A. J. Davey. Patents were also applied for in several foreign countries. This satisfied the War Office, and as the new equipment was considered to be such an advance over previous models, 1,300 sets of the Mills–Burrowes equipment were ordered for extended Service trials.

In the belief that the results of the British trial would be given added weight if the equipment were also tried in India under what would amount to Active Service conditions, the company secured an order for fifty sets from the India Office in London. Wise then got permission for the company to observe the trials and persuaded the other directors to allow him to go to India at the company's expense. He went over-land to Marseilles, embarking there for Alexandria and stopping for a week at Cairo where he secured a small trial order for the Mills–Burrowes equipment through an introduction by Mr Davey, who had worked for some years in Egypt.

Wise arrived in Calcutta in January 1907—ahead of the trial equipment. He calculated that he would have time to pay a quick visit to Australia before it arrived (bear in mind all his travelling had to be done by sea!). He stayed there only a few days, enough to pave the way for a future visit on the strength of the British and Indian trials.

On his return to Calcutta he succeeded in getting an interview with Lord Kitchener to receive his instructions about the regiments selected for carrying out the trials. Lord Kitchener decreed that ten sets of equipment should go to each of the following: the Wiltshire Regiment at Dagshai, the 36th Sikhs at Rawalpindi, the West Yorkshire Regiment at Murree, the 4th Gurkhas at Bakloh, and the Rifle Brigade at Chaubuttia. Detailed orders were issued by General Mahon, the Director of Ordnance in India, and it was arranged that Wise should follow up the trials at intervals.

General Mahon was keen on the idea of manufacturing the equipment in India, if it was adopted, and discussions took place with the Elgin Mills Company of Cawnpore. It was then found that Indian cotton would be unsuitable for making webbing equipment of the quality demanded by the British War Office because it was of very short staple. Instead, the Elgin Mills Company were appointed sole agents in India.

Wise visited the various stations where the trials were being held and while he was in Simla he was fortunate in meeting Major Goodenough, a British Army officer attached to the State of Gwalior. He arranged for the equipment to be demonstrated to the Maharajah, and substantial orders were later received from Gwalior through the Elgin Mills Company.

Although there was a tinge of the old prejudice in favour of leather in one or two of them, the reports from the regiments were on the whole excellent, especially the one from Major (later Colonel) C. Douglas Roe of the 4th Gurkhas, a keen soldier who proved to be a very good friend of the Mills Equipment Company because of his enthusiasm for webbing equipment compared with leather in hot climates like India. In fact the great advantage of web equipment was that it was not affected by prolonged rains or spells of torrid heat, so that it was just as serviceable and efficient in tropical and frigid countries as it was in temperate climates.

Before leaving for home William Wise was summoned to Military Headquarters at Simla for an interview with Lord Kitchener which had been arranged by Colonel William Birdwood, Military Secretary to Lord Kitchener (later to become Lieutenant-General Birdwood, commander of the Anzac Forces at Gallipoli). It turned out to be an exceedingly high-level meeting with four major-generals in attendance, and its purpose was to decide whether to approve or reject webbing equipment on the basis of their reports. After seeing the difference in condition between the old leather equipment and the new webbing after identical service in the field, and hearing an explanation by Wise of the minor improvements that had been suggested as a results of the trials, Lord Kitchener solemnly asked each general his opinion in turn. One after the other replied 'I approve, Sir'. After a further brief discussion Lord Kitchener gave instructions for the reports to be sent immediately to the War Office with his personal endorsement.

Meanwhile the reports on the official trials carried out in England had also been favourable and eventually in December 1907 the Army Council met to reach a final decision on the question of adopting webbing equipment for the British Army and Imperial Forces. Arthur Davey and William Wise were invited to attend this important meeting and answer any questions of detail, but a decision had to be deferred to a further meeting because an additional item, the entrenching tool, which had just been devised in India, had to be accommodated in the equipment. All went well on the second occasion and the equipment was finally approved, much to the delight of all concerned.

It had taken four years of sustained effort to rehabilitate webbing equipment after its eclipse by leather following the Boer War, and the moment of triumph came when it was demonstrated to HM King Edward VII at Buckingham Palace on 30 January 1908. The next day nearly every newspaper in the land carried a report and illustration of a soldier wearing the equipment, which was officially known as the Pattern 1908 Web Infantry Equipment.

The acceptance of webbing equipment by the War Office, delayed as it was for several years, completely vindicated William Lindsey's original enterprise in coming to England in 1899. In the same year, 1908, he himself gained control of the Mills Woven Cartridge Company of Worcester, Massachusetts, which had replaced the old Mills–Orndorff company in 1905.

The first order for 15,000 sets of the new equipment was received from the War Office on 3 March 1908, three days after the company moved to larger offices at 72 Victoria Street. But this was only the beginning—the company were told that the Army would need about 90,000 sets a year. This was far more than the maximum output of the small factory at Stoke Newington, so a freehold site for a new factory was purchased a couple of miles away at Fountayne Road, Tottenham. On the advice of Francis Stevenson, who had developed a great liking for the company, a Dundee architect was engaged to design a purpose-built factory. (One of his young draughtsmen on the job, David Stiven, was persuaded to join the company when the building was finished as an assistant to the head weaver and learnt the job so well that he became the company's textile manager.)

Additional looms were ordered from America, sewing machines from the Singer company, and the latest types of presses for making the brass fittings. By the end of 1908 all was ready for the factory to be formally opened on 20 December by the chairman the Hon Arthur Davey. Eight days later Francis Stevenson joined the Mills board. The productive capacity of the new factory was 2,500 sets of equipment a week, which was considered adequate for the gradual re-equipment of the British Home Forces, and the factory was soon running at its full output to meet the contracts from the War Office.

Meanwhile the company helped in the preparation of a military handbook on the correct way to use the equipment to ensure a comfortable and well-balanced load. To be absolutely certain there would be no complaints arising from misuse of the equipment, a representative was sent—with War Office permission—to demonstrate the equipment at every infantry depot and barracks in the British Isles. It was found that the main problem was to get the soldier to realise that the right position in which to carry a load on his back was on a level with the waist belt and not high up on the shoulders. This propaganda exercise, which was thought to be rather extravagant at the time, proved to be well worth while, and the '08 equipment became universally regarded as the best and most comfortable outfit for the foot soldier.

It was only to be expected that the wholesale switch to webbing equipment would create difficulties for the firms engaged in supplying leather equipment—indeed, two of them went out of business altogether. Another decided to swim with the tide and offered to place at the Mills Company's disposal the connections they had built up with the Territorial Army Associations set up under the national scheme launched by Lord Haldane. They were given the Mills agency for the associations outside London. This arrangement came at a convenient time because Mills had decided to introduce, for the benefit of the smaller county associations, a modified form of the 1908 equipment with cartridge pockets for 90 rounds instead of the usual 150. It was lighter and cheaper, and consequently sold by the thousands.

The City of London and County of London associations ordered the full-size equipment, and the London Scottish were so pleased with it that they had a shot at the London to Brighton record with a platoon in full marching order. Young Lethern was asked by the adjutant to go along and make sure the equipment was properly assembled and adjusted before the platoon set off, and received a letter of thanks and a silver cigarette case for his trouble. The platoon completed the march in 16 hr 40 min, which was some form of record.

It was only to be expected, too, that some agitation should develop on account of the monopoly position Mills found themselves in resulting from the special plant they used and the patent covering the equipment. Moreover, the Government were not too keen on having the manufacture of webbing equipment centred in London. Another company, M. Wright & Sons of Leicester, was therefore brought into competition with Mills, who were asked to teach them some of the special weaving processes. Mills continued to make all the metal fittings, both for their own production and for Wright's. However, Mills succeeded in getting a royalty on every set of equipment made outside during the rest of the sixteen-year term of the patent.

This dramatic photograph of firemen in RFD Mills Equipment aluminised heat-resistant suits fighting an aircraft fire was taken by Jim Hunt, resident photographer and head of the RFD Group's technical publications department. It won for him the trophy for 'The Best Black-and-White Photograph for General Use' in the *Financial Times* 1971 Industrial Photographic Competition

(*left*) Kenneth Kerr's attempt to row across the Atlantic single-handed ended when his 13ft boat *Bass Conqueror* capsized in violent seas 700 miles off the Canadian coastline. He took to his RFD Seasava 4-man liferaft and 30 hours later transferred to a larger liferaft dropped to him by an aircraft of the Royal Canadian Air Force, which directed a ship to his rescue

(*below*) One of four survivors being lifted from their RFD 8MM liferaft by a Sea King helicopter of 824 Royal Naval Air Squadron after the coaster *Greta-C* foundered in heavy seas off the south-west of England on 8 September 1974. (Photographs from HMS *Ark Royal* published by permission of the Royal Navy)

Until the outbreak of war in August 1914 the Mills Company worked like beavers to expand their sales abroad. The various arrangements included direct exports through agents, licences for manufacturing complete sets of equipment or individual items, like haversacks, and the formation of subsidiary manufacturing companies for which the plant was shipped from England. In many cases the Great War intervened before the plans came to fruition. The countries they campaigned in were Italy, Portugal, Spain, Germany, Belgium, France, Romania, Bulgaria, Serbia, Turkey, Russia, Brazil and Peru. The introduction of web equipment to the Turkish, Bulgarian and Serbian armies was negotiated during a tour of the Balkans by Kenneth Lindsey, William's son, who joined the board on 28 May 1913 (and was later to become chairman).

Negotiations with the War Department of Russia had started in 1908 through a US Army officer who was the company's representative. In 1910 a Russian company was formed, La Société d'Equipment Russe (Systéme Mills), but before it could start to operate the equipment had to be entered for a competition to determine the equipment most worthy of adoption by the Russian Army. The Mills entry won, and Davey and Wise went to St Petersburg and arranged for the company to be represented on the sales side by the firm of Wossidlo & Company. Edward Allen followed them up to supervise the installation of the plant, but the beginning of the war overtook the project and the machinery was never seen again.

The company made another attempt to operate in France, mainly because of the encouragement they received from a retired French Army colonel, Paul Bruzon, who was an enthusiastic supporter of the Pattern 1908 equipment, to which he added special bits to suit the French Army requirements. Lengthy trials were carried out and in January 1914 a French company, Société le Coton File, was formed with the intention of setting up a factory in Paris to manufacture the Mills–Bruzon equipment. There was every hope of getting this adopted when the war put an end to the plans.

Given an earlier start of the negotiations (which actually began in 1913), units of the German Army might well have been equipped with Mills webbing equipment at the start of the Great War. Contact was made with the firm of Wollheim & Osenbach of Berlin, who had good connections with the Army and Navy departments and they succeeded in getting an order for 500 sets of equipment for the Navy and a smaller lot for the Army, both for trials. A complete German soldier's outfit was sent to the Mills factory as a guide. A brown shade of colour was specified, presumably to resemble leather, and the harshness of the dye gave a lot of trouble with the stitching. However, the sets were delivered on time and they were actually on trial when the war started. (In the event the German soldier continued to use the existing leather equipment, which carried 120 cartridges with a reserve of 30 rounds stowed somewhat inconveniently in his knapsack. He was thus at a considerable disadvantage in fire power compared with the British soldier, who had 150 cartridges in his web equipment with a further 100 rounds immediately available in an emergency bandolier slung across his chest.)

Good progress was made in supplying the 1908 Pattern equipment to the Dominions and Colonies with the notable exception of Canada, where it was strongly disliked by General Sir Sam Hughes, Commander-in-Chief of the Canadian Army, who insisted on using leather Oliver equipment. William Wise got to hear that Sir Sam was coming to London, so he asked him for an appointment. He was told to present himself at 7.30 am one morning at the Savoy Hotel, in company with Major Burrowes. Wise put on the fully loaded equipment—marching order with 150 rounds of ammunition—and actually stood on his head and 'walked' across the room on his hands to prove the compact balancing features of the equipment. The demonstration was successful enough, but no headway could be made with the general.

Wise continued to plug away. Shortly after the war started he met Sir Sam Hughes in Ottawa and pointed out the difficulties that would arise in supply when the Canadian regiments went overseas and were brigaded with British infantry using different types of personal equipment. The general was still unimpressed; nevertheless as soon as the Canadian Forces reached England they were re-equipped with the Pattern 1908 web equipment. Lethern was sent down to Salisbury Plain in the depth of winter to instruct Canadian and French Canadian troops how to assemble and get the best out of the equipment.

The declaration of war on 4 August 1914 caught the Mills company in a curious situation. The re-fitting of the Army with webbing equipment had recently been completed and the factory was working with only a nucleus of staff. All at once more workpeople had to be taken on to resume production and plans drawn up to enlarge the factory. Fortunately there was plenty of land next to the factory at Tottenham, which in 1911 had been extended to almost double its original capacity (it now covered more than 42,000 sq ft). No time was lost in acquiring more land and starting building—in fact work began before the end of August. The first factory was now called No 1 and the new one No 2 (nearly 20,000 sq ft). Two months later No 3 factory began to go up, covering about 40,000 sq ft. In the meantime orders were placed for a large number of cartridge belt looms to be built at Worcester, Mass, and sent to London as quickly as possible. Edward Allen, the factory manager, trained new employees till there were 2,000 on the payroll, and he organised the whole expansion so efficiently that in less than nine months the total output reached 20,000 sets of equipment a week— nearly ten times the capacity of the original factory. The company were considerably helped in this period of expansion by the enormous credit given to them by Francis Stevenson, the Dundee dyers.

All this equipment was required by the fighting troops—there was nothing left over for training purposes. To meet this need, the Government ordered about a million sets of Pattern 1908 equipment with the basic parts made of leather. The orders went to contractors all over England as well as to American manufacturers. When the men went overseas the regulation Pattern 1908 webbing equipment was issued to them. The War Office agreed to pay the Mills Company a substantial sum for the use of their patents.

One of the strongholds of leather equipment was the regulation officer's Sam Browne belt, which had a pistol case and ammunition pouch carried on the belt, and field-glass case, haversack and water-bottle carrier with slings across the chest added for service requirements. The complete outfit made the officer horribly conspicuous in action and in the early days of war many were picked off by snipers. For their own safety officers were forced to use the infantryman's web equipment, even with the pack, until the Mills web equipment for officers was eventually adopted. Thousands of sets were sold to officers individually and through military tailors.

In October 1914 a serious complaint was received from GHQ in France that ammunition was being lost from the three lower pockets of the left-hand cartridge carrier of the 1908 equipment, owing to the snap fasteners in the flaps becoming accidentally opened when the soldier was leaning against the parapet of the trench to fire his rifle. The message came through to the factory one afternoon, and by the late evening Lethern had made a prototype carrier with the three lower flaps fitted with a sliding strap which enabled the pockets to be easily filled but prevented the clips falling out of the pockets when the flaps were unfastened. The next morning Wise went to the War Office with a set of equipment and once again put on his act of walking on his hands across the room, demonstrating that with the three lower flaps unfastened, ammunition could not be lost from the cartridge carrier. Instructions were immediately given to use the ammunition-retaining strap on all future supplies of left-hand cartridge carriers. This was the last that was heard of the problem—indeed no complaints of any sort were made about the Pattern 1908 web infantry equipment during the rest of its life of twenty-nine years until the 1937 Pattern was adopted.

A month before the Armistice brought the war to an end on 11 November 1918, the Mills Company lost one of its chief architects in the death of the Hon Arthur Davey, who had been chairman of the company since its formation in 1906. In February 1917 he had resigned to take up the position of Deputy Director of Army Contracts at the War Office. On 10 October 1918 he was returning from an official visit to Ireland in the ill-fated SS *Leinster* when it was torpedoed by a German submarine in the Irish Sea. Arthur Davey was drowned while attempting to go below to collect his official documents. A memorial service was held at St Margaret's, Westminster, and the church was filled to overflowing with his many friends and Government officials.

As a result of a meeting between Wise and Lieutenant-General Sir Arthur Sloggett, who had been Director General of the Army Medical Service throughout the war, it was decided to invite Sir Arthur to join the board because of his long connection with the Army and the advice he could give on developments in equipment design, particularly from the medical point of view. He readily accepted and in December 1918 was elected chairman.

Four years later, on 25 November 1922, the founder of the company, William Lindsey, died suddenly in the United States in his sixty-fifth year. His death, coupled with the poor outlook for obtaining orders for military equipment in the slump of the early 1920s, determined the American shareholders of the British company to liquidate it and reform it in May 1923 for the manufacture of domestic as well as military articles. Various things were designed in webbing for the commercial market, and a certain amount of success was achieved in the sale of golf bags through one of the big sports-goods dealers. But military webbing equipment remained the company's mainstay.

A newcomer to the board in 1922, Major T. Lethaby OBE, who had been in charge of accoutrement requirements for the Army during the war and had finished his job as Director of Disposals of Surplus Stores, now joined William Wise as joint managing director. A few years later, on 10 November 1928, Wise resigned from the company and returned to the United States. He had got into personal financial difficulties owing to some imprudent speculations, and had to sell his shares in Mills Equipment. This was a sad ending to an association that went right back to the early years of the century. He was the first managing director of the company when it was formed in 1906, and since that time he had shown great enterprise and energy, as we have seen, in pressing the merits of webbing equipment in influential quarters all over the world. Major Lethaby now became sole managing director. A year later, in 1929, Sir Arthur Sloggett died—after having carried a sniper's bullet near his heart for thirty-one years since the Battle of Omdurman in 1898. His place as chairman was taken by Kenneth Lindsey.

For most of the period between the wars the Pattern 1908 web equipment remained regulation wear for the British infantry, but variations were produced incorporating cartridge cases adjustable at the back and straps to enable the pack to be carried like a rucksack. This found favour with the Royal Navy for officers and petty officers, and was adopted by the Royal Air Force for airmen and NCOs in 1925. A large business was also done in renovating surplus Government stock and selling thousands of sets to foreign countries as far apart as Ethiopia and Peru. A team of workpeople was employed sorting, grading and finally reconditioning every item with a special preparation—applied hot—which was made by James Hamilton & Sons of Dundee and resulted in the articles being rendered virtually as good as new. Although batches of individual parts were being continually sold, it was the company's policy to conserve complete sets as far as possible, and these stocks were to prove a godsend in the early days of the Second World War when thousands of troops evacuated from the beaches at Dunkirk returned without their equipment. The Mills Company were able to supply 30,000 complete sets of Pattern 1908 equipment immediately as a stop-gap.

In 1932 the whole question of clothing and personal equipment of the British soldier was reviewed by the Braithwaite Committee and resulted in the eventual introduction of the battle dress and the Pattern

1937 web equipment, which Mills developed in collaboration with the Royal Ordnance Depot at Didcot. The merit of this equipment was its versatility—it could be varied to suit infantrymen carrying rifles or Bren guns, and by officers and others carrying pistols only. The rucksack method was developed for carrying either the haversack in battle order or the one-piece pack in marching order simply by interchanging the shoulder straps. The first substantial contract was placed with the Mills Company in April 1938, and this was followed by large orders to re-equip the Forces. It was not long before the equipment was also adopted by the Dominion Governments.

In January 1938 experiments were started with a new design of legging for the Army which developed into the web anklet for use with battle dress. This was made in enormous quantities, in khaki for the Army and blue-grey for the RAF.

The period between the wars also saw the beginning of the Mills Company's business in supplying safety equipment to the aircraft world. In 1928 a contract was received from the Air Ministry for making the Sutton pilot's safety harness, and within two years the company was firmly established in this field. A great improvement in the construction and strength of the harness was achieved by eliminating leather facings as a means of reinforcing the straps which were fastened across the pilot's chest. Instead, hidden flexible steel strips, anchored to the main straps in a special way, were found so successful in increasing the strength of the straps that the invention was patented and subsequently adopted by the Air Ministry. The Sutton-type harness remained standard equipment in the Royal Air Force until the introduction in 1938 of the Q-type harness which was designed by Albert Lethern of Mills Equipment in conjunction with Captain Frederick Wigley of the Air Ministry (and in collaboration with A. S. Quirico as regards the 4-point release). Many thousand harnesses were manufactured by Mills for Fighter and Bomber Command aircraft throughout the Second World War. From 1931 onwards the company developed a range of seat belts-cum-harnesses at the request of the Air Ministry.

As the country prepared against the threat of war, the Mills Company increased its capacity to meet the increasing demand for its products. At Tottenham a fourth factory (a four-storey building) was completed early in 1937, and in April 1939 the original No 1 factory, which had been sold to a local boot and shoe manufacturer in 1921 when military orders were at a low ebb, was bought back again to bring up the total area of the four-factory complex to 120,000sq ft. Then another little factory nearby in Harold Road was acquired and equipped as a finishing plant. But more capacity was needed when war broke out and this was found a few miles away at Walthamstow, where a large building (later called South Mill) was rented from Achille Serre, the dry cleaners, and equipped with the latest automatic looms, while a new building (North Mill) was put up nearby on land purchased in November 1939 at Blackhorse Lane. Soon afterwards another building was bought at Edmonton trading estate and fitted out with 900 sewing machines as an assembly and finishing section. When all these plants were at full stretch in the summer of 1940 the payroll rose to nearly 7,000.

On 7 September 1940 the Germans, having failed to crush the RAF in the Battle of Britain, switched their attack to night raids on London. The 'blitz' continued for seventy-five successive nights. On 23 September the Nos 3 and 4 factories at Tottenham were destroyed, except for a small section including the important test room. All the company's records, including the wages sheets, went up in the flames and on the next pay day the staff were paid from the clerks' memories of what they earned. They had to queue up at desks and tables set up in the street, and there was not a single complaint. About 2,000 operatives were thrown out of work and the damage was estimated at nearly a quarter-of-a-million pounds. The company were particularly grieved at the loss of the shrinking plant, which was one of the prides of Tottenham. It was the custom for every width of webbing and all woven items like cartridge carriers to be shrunk in hot water, transferred to steam tanks, and then dried in airing cupboards. These processes had to stop because the plant in No 3 factory was completely destroyed. A licence to re-erect the plant was refused, so wasteful 'cutting-allowances' to compensate for the natural shrinkage of materials had to be introduced.

Three days later a further disaster smote the company when a bomb fell on a storehouse rented at Edmonton and very large stocks of fabrics were completely destroyed. A month later Nos 1 and 2 factories at Tottenham were slightly damaged and on 8 December No 2 was hit again, fortunately with only minor damage to plant and machinery.

The reduction in output caused by these raids was so serious that the Ministry started to build up a Narrow Fabrics Directorate in Manchester in an attempt to get alternative supplies of webbing from other textile firms. Mills Equipment had close connections with Manchester through their major yarn suppliers, Stott & Sons, and just before the war they had fortunately placed a very large futures order on cotton at 9¼d. By the time they began to use it during the war the market price was two or three times as high.

So far the large single-storey assembly building on the Edmonton trading estate had escaped the attention of the Germans, although it was right in the middle of a heavy raid on 20 January 1941. But its good luck did not hold and on the night of 19 March the factory was burnt out so completely that it was impossible to retrieve any of the 900 sewing machines or other plant. The loss of production was partly made good by the other finishing plants at Tottenham and Dagenham, where a large building had been leased in December to make up for the loss of finishing production at Tottenham.

Even then the Luftwaffe had not done with Mills Equipment. On 19 February 1945—three months before the end of the war in Europe—a V-2 rocket came to earth at two o'clock in the afternoon between the North and South Mills at Walthamstow, devastating the factory belonging to W. B. Brawn & Company and killing several people. The two Mills factories suffered badly enough, the roofs being lifted, windows smashed and machinery damaged. No one was killed, but unhappily several of the employees were injured. As it was the depth of winter, the first essential was to protect the building with tarpaulins, after which a start was made on clearing up the debris. Within forty-eight hours weaving was resumed, the operatives working in overcoats because there was no heating and wearing steel helmets in case broken glass was dislodged from the shattered roof. This was typical of the stoical spirit of the workpeople throughout the company—and indeed the country—all through the war. They carried on working under trying conditions with constant interruptions by air-raid warnings, which very often reached the danger-signal stage that meant stopping work immediately and retreating to the air-raid shelters.

In spite of these difficult working conditions the Mills factories in North London turned out a vast amount of webbing articles of various kinds during the Second World War. Contracts were received for a million sets of equipment at a time, to be followed in due course by a repeat order. Mills could never produce enough. The balance of the demand was met by other companies, some of which remained as competitors after the war while others went back to their original business. In addition to the Pattern 1937 equipment for the British and

Allied Forces, the company supplied large quantities of the USA/1910 equipment for the American Army and in 1943 designed and produced the lightweight Pattern 1944 web equipment in vat-dyed jungle-green and rot-proofed fabric for the troops in the Far East. On top of this they manufactured many other webbing items such as portable food containers, aerial gear bags and cases for mine detectors.

Talks with the Americans about supplying them with webbing equipment revealed that the pockets of their standard webbing equipment were stitched. When they were asked if they would prefer to have the woven pockets of the British Pattern 1937 equipment, some of the older officers were quite amused and said 'Why, we used to have those.' It appeared that woven pockets had been dropped because it was no longer economic to make them in America.

The organisation and expansion of the factories during the war was the responsibility of Gerald Fairlie, the works manager, who was peculiarly well suited for the job because his early training had been as a structural engineer. This enabled him to deal rapidly with the effects of bomb and fire damage and get the factories going again with the minimum of delay.

In view of the important role he was destined to play, it is worth digressing for a moment to trace Gerald Fairlie's career with the company up to this point. He had been brought in way back in 1926 as assistant to the then works manager, Edward Allen, the American technician who had come over with William Lindsey to start the business in 1899 and who had been appointed a director in 1922. Allen had just lost his two right-hand men—one of them handled the wages and was found to have been embezzling money for years, and the other, who was in charge of assembly, had been playing fast and loose with the company and decided the time had come to get out before he was thrown out. Allen himself was ill at the time, and he desperately needed someone to come in and sort out the factories (which were losing money) and to introduce some scientific methods of accountancy and costing. Although Fairlie had no qualifications as regards accountancy, textiles, making up or metal work, he had an orderly mind that appealed to Allen and as a structural engineer was equipped to get the factories in good physical shape. A new production man was taken on but did not prove satisfactory so Fairlie promoted a youngster named Leonard Oliver in his place. (He rose to the opportunity splendidly, and in course of time was to become a key asset to the company in the takeover negotiations with the RFD Group.) As his lieutenant on the administrative side Fairlie was fortunate in having another outstanding young man in Brian Thom at his disposal.

At the beginning of the Second World War the running of the Mills Company had taken a rather peculiar turn. Kenneth Lindsey, the chairman, and Albert Lethern, who was appointed director and managing director in 1941 on the resignation of Major Lethaby, moved out of Westminster with the headquarters staff and stationed themselves at Lethaby's home, the Old Rectory House, on Wimbledon Common, overflowing into the place next door. (Lethaby himself spent most of his time in the United States.) From then onwards they ventured across London to the factories in Tottenham, Walthamstow and Edmonton only once or twice a year, Lindsey to distribute prizes or presents at Christmas or some other special occasion and Lethern to discuss sales, for which he was responsible. They were content to leave the management of the factories to Fairlie while the headquarters confined themselves to finance and dealings with the War Office. 'I produced the costs,' Fairlie recalls, 'but what they did with them was their business. If they didn't like the price they used to say "You can't take our on-costs and you'll have to put them on something else." I said "You can't ignore the on-cost, it's there, it's not a fictitious figure I've invented." And so for many years we made a loss on some items. Eventually they started to put the on-cost in their prices again, and we made a profit once more.'

As soon as the war ended, the break-clause in all contracts came into force and the production of war equipment ceased. The company's activity contracted until there was only one factory employing about 300 people, instead of seven factories with a payroll of 7,000. During the war the Government had installed at their own expense literally hundreds of new looms in the company's weaving sheds and hundreds of brand-new sewing machines in their outlying factories. Mills were hopeful that they would be allowed to buy all this new equipment, but the Government refused to sell. Len Oliver bitterly remembers what happened:

> They sent in a firm of scrap metal merchants to break them up with sledge hammers. It broke my heart—brand new machines, especially the brand-new looms, which cost an awful lot of money. The thinking evidently was 'Nobody is going to make a profit out of them except the Government, so we'd rather smash them up.' So that's what they did.

164

Fairlie now found himself faced with an utterly different labour situation that was to have the gravest consequences for the company, as he explained:

Since the days of our expansion in the First World War we had always been able to draw in people from the neighbouring streets. Mr Allen trained them for the various sections, and the moment we were short of work we just paid them off. They went home—not particularly unhappy, because their husbands were mostly in work anyway—and when we wanted more people we only had to give the word and there were floods of them at our gates. They were nearly all women or girls, and a few boys who learnt to press parts in the metal section. So a flow of local labour was available to us up to the beginning of the Second World War—and then I was able to get the people who were being thrown out of other businesses.

After the war it was a very different matter. Few of them wanted to come back when business revived—they knew that, apart from a nucleus of permanent staff, it was only spasmodic work, there was no security in it, and they naturally looked for other jobs. It was also very hard work; the stuff was heavy to handle, the machines were heavy, and the noise in the loom sheds was terrible—you couldn't hear yourself speak.

There was a change too—and for the worse—in the kind of orders for webbing we were receiving. We started to be asked to meet small orders—masses of them—for straps for this and bags for that. Mr Lethern wanted every order to be accepted in the hope that the sprats would catch some mackerels. He used to come down to Tottenham for a few days at a time to develop these small items in the sample room. The sales department accordingly kept accepting orders in the hope that we would be able to meet the deliveries they had quoted (without consulting us). As it was quite impossible for us to take on the extra labour to get the quick expansion in production needed, the order book became jammed and the company was anything up to a year in arrears with deliveries. Our strength had always been that if any country came along with an urgent order we could offer them quick delivery, but without the flexibility of labour we used to enjoy this was no longer possible.

Another snag with these special articles was that there was no justification for carrying on production and building up stocks when we were slack, as there was with complete sets of web equipment. A big proportion of our business became devoted to these small orders, and they couldn't bear the overheads of a big company that had to keep its factories going with its plant largely idle. So the company was getting uneconomic.

The position was only partly relieved by an attempt to diversify the company's range of products. With the aid of a sales force a big business was done for a time in supplying various kinds of bags—travel bags, cosmetic bags, printed plastic bags—to the leading London stores and to Boots, Timothy Whites and other shops in the provinces, but it did not last long.

In 1946 an agreement had been reached with J. W. Wood (Elastic Webbing Manufacturers) of Stoughton, Mass, USA for the licence to use their shuttleless high-speed needle loom for the manufacture of narrow webbings and elastics, narrow fabrics from $\frac{1}{2}$in to 18in wide for web equipment and other articles, canvas as wide as 35in for awnings, and lamp wicks. A prototype loom was sent over from America and L. S. Irvine, an experienced technician who had been with Mills since 1913, got to work developing and improving certain features. A large number of looms was eventually built and installed with the necessary auxiliary plant at the Harold Road factory at Tottenham. The trade in narrow fabrics and elastics was found to be already over-crowded with firms established in cheap labour areas and with experienced salesmen and the right contacts. Great store was set on developing a large business in lamp wicks for oil heaters, but this was ruined by the influx of immigrants who used them in every room of their crowded quarters—and inevitably knocked them over. The expected boom in lamp wicks consequently failed to materialise. Quite a good trade in canvas for deck chairs was done for a while, but the most successful product of the new looms was bedding tape used in making mattresses—Mills turned out millions and millions of yards. Perhaps the main benefit derived from this new development was the extra business the company were able to do with RFD and GQ Parachutes, for whom the narrow webbing was particularly useful.

A trade mark was required to differentiate these products from Mills military equipment, and the word CEMRON was registered. The factory was given the same name. When the No 4 factory was reconstructed as a two-storey building in 1952, the Harold Road premises were closed and the work transferred to No 4, a part of which was thereafter called CEMRON Works.

Fortunately there was still a small demand for complete sets of military web equipment. This was partly because the British Government had supplied the Pattern 1937 web equipment to Allied forces during the war, and the Army Departments of various countries (notably Belgium, Denmark, Holland, Luxembourg and Norway) continued to equip their troops with it afterwards, practically without any change in the design. The exception was Denmark, where much discussion took place over the design of a new type of cover for the water bottle before a substantial contract was placed with Mills in 1948. But the changes required by the Danes did not end there. In the next few years a modified version of the haversack was devised and a new basic pouch that could be used to carry a wide variety of items— cartridge magazines of two lengths, loose cartridges, grenades, signal pistol cartridges in a container, a pistol in a special holder, binoculars, or spare parts for automatic rifles. A unique feature was a 'trap' flap at the bottom to allow grenades or cartridges to be easily extracted, over- coming the difficulty of reaching inside from the top of the rather deep pouch. Kenneth Lindsey and Albert Lethern went over to Copenhagen in 1950 and clinched a large order for the new pouch. This was followed by the supply of fabrics and fittings for several articles of equipment for bulk assembly by contractors in Denmark.

Lethern was in his element working out the modifications to the equipment and he found a fellow enthusiast in Major Anton N. Hvidt, the secretary of the Danish personal equipment committee. As Fairlie put it: 'Lethern had an almost childlike faith in the beauty of the web equipment.' The ingenuity he brought to its design and production, with all the various appendages for special weapons and accessories, was eventually recognised by the award of the OBE.

Good business was also done with the Belgians, who had adopted the Pattern 1908 equipment in the First World War and had used Mills equipment ever since. Outside Europe orders were received for the Pattern 1937 equipment from Iraq, Pakistan, Burma and other emer- gent countries, while the Israeli Army was equipped with the Pattern 1937 equipment modified to incorporate the back-strap balancing feature of the 1944 equipment. On the financial side the Government helped with export guarantees.

So far the Government had depended to a great extent on the Mills company for the design and development of web equipment, but in 1958 the Ministry of Defence decided to set up their own design depart- ment and discontinue their association with the company. The first fruit of the new establishment at Colchester was the Pattern 1958 web equipment, which was largely based on the Pattern 1944 equip- ment designed by Mills. In the event, the company were involved in approving the design of the new pattern and vetting the methods of manufacture and assembly. It was to become the standard equipment of the armed forces not only in Britain but in most countries of the world.

And now a new aspect of the labour situation began to be felt. In Fairlie's words: 'Many of our staff, who had worked wonderfully for us, were getting old. They were mostly pensionable, and we couldn't get young people to work with them. We got into a dead end there—we were a stagnant business in an unsatisfactory location.'

For some time Fairlie had realised that there was no future for the company in its present form. 'I was seventy and Lindsey and Lethern were both in their eighties, and we were the only directors.' Fairlie had wanted to bring Oliver and Thom on to the board, to which they would have made an excellent contribution, but Lindsey would not hear of it. (Lethern had worked for the company for thirty-five years before he was made a director.) Kenneth Lindsey had come to look on the company as very much his own property—it was a private company anyway, and he had control.

Then there was the question of finance, over which Lindsey kept a tight but not very sophisticated grip. When he was made a director in 1942 Fairlie discovered that the company's considerable reserves had been allowed to accumulate in the bank on current account 'because they liked to feel they could always draw it out'. It took a great deal of persuasion to convince Lindsey that they could actually make more profit from the interest on the money if it were put on deposit account than they made in the company itself. Years earlier, before the Wall Street crash, Lindsey had wanted to invest all the reserves on the New York stock market. The other directors had luckily over-ruled him, and he had been very sore about it ever since.

At the beginning of 1968 Fairlie decided to set the ball rolling himself. 'As we couldn't expand, I began to look around for a buyer whom I could recommend.' He had good contacts in the textile industry—he had been deputy chairman of the Webbing Manufacturers Association and on the committee of the Textile Narrow Fabrics Council during the war—so he got in touch with Small & Parkes, Thomas French and John Carr in the hope that they might be interested in taking over not only the weaving side but the making-up and the metal components as well—he wanted to keep the place either running or disposed of as a going concern. But though they might have considered buying the goodwill of the company, they were not willing to take over the factories and staff.

Then I found that John Hayward of Arthur Hart & Sons, Crewkerne, the Somerset group, was prepared to take over our looms and most of our textile stocks, which were considerable. By this time the word had gone round the trade that the company was looking for buyers and out of the blue I had a visit from Alan Wylie, the managing director of the RFD Group. After going round the works he offered to take a certain amount of our textile stock, our sewing and making-up machines, and our metal and metal fitting stocks, which were very high. Above all RFD would take on the assembly, provided they could have Len Oliver. They had room to accommodate the business at their parachute factory at Waterlooville, and there was labour available, which we hadn't got.

Indeed, as we have seen, the utilisation of the largely under-employed GQ factory at Waterlooville was the main object of the exercise from RFD's point of view.

Kenneth Lindsey and Albert Lethern had no alternative to suggest and reluctantly agreed to Fairlie's plans. A straightforward sale of the looms and textile stock was made to Arthur Hart, and on 2 December 1968 contractual arrangements for the purchase by the RFD Group of 'the name, goodwill and certain other assets of the Mills Equipment Company' were concluded. The engineering equipment and tools were moved from Tottenham to Godalming and the sewing and assembling machinery to Waterlooville. At the same time the Mills Equipment Company took over the safety and industrial equipment which GQ Parachutes had developed.

Gerald Fairlie retired officially at the beginning of 1969 but stayed on for a few months to complete the sale of the factories at Tottenham. For Kenneth Lindsey the loss of his business was an emotional shock from which he never recovered. He died a few months after the company was sold. Albert Lethern, suddenly deprived of his life-long interest, died shortly afterwards.

CHAPTER ELEVEN

A CHAPTER BEST FORGOTTEN

In the process of integrating Mills Equipment into the Group's operations, it occurred to the board that the time had come to reorganise the structure of the Group as a whole. Discussion of ways and means of carrying this out went on all through 1969. In the end it was decided that merging the three manufacturing subsidiaries, the RFD Company, GQ Parachutes and Mills Equipment, in a single trading company would enable the administrative and other common functions of all three to be centralised and rationalised, thereby—it was claimed—'improving efficiency, reducing operating costs and releasing capital for other purposes'. A new company, RFD–GQ Limited, was therefore formed on 1 April 1970 to amalgamate the three separate businesses and run them as one company comprising five divisions: a Survival and Inflatables Division, a Parachute Division, a Mills Equipment Division, an Engineering Division, and an Industrial Safety Division. An NCR 100 computer was leased and installed at the central administrative headquarters in Godalming, but because the necessary ancillary software was not available at the same time, it only made more clerical work, instead of less.

The attempt to centralise the administrative and trading functions of such diverse manufacturing operations was doomed to failure from the start. Arthur Dickinson, the managing director of GQ Parachutes at the time, summed up the feelings of those who had to try and make it work when he recalled: 'It was the biggest mistake they could possibly have made. It was an absolute shambles.'

In the same month of 1970 Charles de Boinville joined the Group board as the chairman-elect. Anton van Beugen Bik, after thirty-one years' extremely valuable service with the company, was finally going to retire in July. In 1968, when he had been due to retire at the age of seventy-one, he had been re-elected as a director and continued as chairman while Alan Wylie became sole managing director. De

Saved! After six days afloat in their 6-man RFD liferaft, the complement of the ketch *One and All* — six men and a woman — were picked up off the coast of New South Wales by HMAS *Otway*, one of Australia's three Oberon class submarines. Shortly after being spotted by a Neptune of the RAAF, they transferred to a larger RFD liferaft in a Lindholme gear dropped by a second Neptune, while an Orion of the RAAF circled overhead to await the arrival of the submarine

(*left*) A GQ 22ft steerable parachute as illustrated was used by 34 year-old David Parchment in setting up a world record of 233 jumps in 18 hours 7 minutes on 18/19 June 1979 at Shobdon, Herefordshire. He broke the record by one jump!

(*right*) Entirely new principles of design and construction are used in the Unicross cargo-carrying parachute, which is made of woven polypropylene material and is of modular construction that can be varied to suit the weight of the load.

Boinville now moved in to acclimatise himself before taking over as non-executive chairman. He had been introduced by Eric Cartwright CBE, who had joined the RFD board as a non-executive director in 1967, through a mutual friend, Derrick Willis of Lazards. (After being on the Cotton Control Board during the war, Cartwright became a well-known figure in the Lancashire cotton trade.) De Boinville had retired early—he had a mild heart attack—from the chairmanship of British Oil & Cake Mills, a subsidiary of Unilever, and he found the RFD non-executive chairmanship a fairly easy commitment compared with his previous position. Nevertheless the change was a challenging contrast for a man who had been accustomed to dealing with many millions of pounds and an enormous staff.

Instead of having to handle a workforce of 17–18,000 people, he found that the average number of employees at RFD was only about 1,500, with a corresponding reduction in the number of managers. Of even greater significance was the totally different scale of corporate organisation. After being used to having the backing of a legal department, a buying department, an engineering department, etc., all laid on at headquarters level, it took some time to understand how a small company like RFD worked.

The main weakness at RFD, in his view, was the dominance of the Group managing director, Alan Wylie, who kept everything under his tight personal control. (This unwillingness to delegate had been an endemic weakness in the top management of RFD since the days of Reginald Dagnall.) The atmosphere at board meetings was not improved by a marked lack of sympathy between Wylie and the Perseverance Mill representatives, in contrast to the welcome given to Wylie's return to the company in 1961 by Alan Noble, the then chairman, who had since retired prematurely for reasons of ill health and had subsequently died.

As the Group managing director, Alan Wylie was made chairman and managing director of the new RFD–GQ Company, and he appointed two joint deputy managing directors in Arthur Dickinson of GQ Parachutes and Robert Cornish, who had been put on the Group board at the beginning of 1970. (Cornish was a chartered secretary who had originally joined RFD as an accountant after the war under a Government scheme for settling ex-officers in industry. He had been made financial controller of the RFD Company in 1967 and a year later was appointed financial director with a seat on the RFD board.)

173

In March 1972 Dickinson left RFD altogether on reaching retiring age, having played an invaluable role in the development of GQ Parachutes since its inception in 1932. The way was now clear for Wylie to persuade the Group board to agree to Cornish taking his own place as managing director of RFD–GQ while he remained as chairman. This, he argued, would leave him free to deal with the wider aspects of Group development as Group managing director, while keeping an eye on RFD–GQ.

In the same month the Group board lost three more stalwarts by the retirement of Philip Lucas, Eric Cartwright and Frank Noble. (Eric Noble had retired from the Group in the previous year, his place being taken by Brian Noble OBE, the youngest son of the founder of Perseverance Mill.)

To compensate for these departures, the Group board received two powerful reinforcements on 1 April 1972. David Mynors was a life-long friend of Charles de Boinville—they had first met on the Rugby field. He had spent the first thirty years of his business career at Courtaulds, for the last twelve of which he had been on the board. But he did not see eye-to-eye with the chairman, Frank (later Lord) Kearton, and retired early. Within a few months Courtauld's loss was Imperial Tobacco's gain. Mynors was given a seat on the board and started up the interest in foods which has subsequently become a major part of the vast Imperial Group's business. The second new director was Guy Gardiner CBE, an aviation consultant with a distinguished career in the aircraft construction industry, who was recommended by Philip Lucas to serve in his place.

As the end of the financial year to 31 March 1973 approached, the Group board became concerned about the quality of management reporting by RFD–GQ, which did not have an integrated management accounting or period accounting system. Various attempts had been made by the RFD–GQ staff to implement better systems, but these had never been carried through to complete fruition with the result that there was a lack of up-to-date reliable cost information.

At the end of March the Group board therefore decided to ask the auditors, Andw W. Barr & Co, to make an urgent survey of the financial reporting and accounting procedures of the company. Their misgivings were borne out when it was learnt on 16 May that RFD–GQ sales in the 1973 financial year were expected to be £575,000 behind budget and overheads were likely to exceed budget by

£100,000. On 1 June Cornish reported that it would be at least four weeks before the draft accounts would be ready. Four days later Andw Barr's report was received, confirming that the system in operation at RFD–GQ was not producing the desired quantity or quality of management information. They recommended that additional accounts department executives should be recruited and that the company should completely review, re-design and document the accounts department procedures and structure so that accurate management reports would be produced on schedule.

This proposal was agreed at the Group board meeting on 11 July, at which Cornish produced the draft accounts of RFD–GQ for the 1972–73 year. These showed that, subject to audit, the profits before tax would be £132,000 against a budget forecast of £310,000. (The audited accounts subsequently increased the profit to £153,000.) At informal discussions before and after the meeting the other directors decided that Cornish would have to be replaced as managing director of RFD–GQ. In the next few days a head-hunting firm was instructed to suggest suitable candidates. At the same time, it was agreed to appoint A. E. (Ted) Queening FCA as financial director of the Group (a new post) with effect from 1 October. Queening had been financial director of the Vokes Limited group, the filtration and engineering specialists at Guildford, who had been recently taken over by Thomas Tilling, and he was to prove a tremendous asset in the next few months of mounting crisis. But he had no idea what he was letting himself in for when he joined.

The Group accounts for the year ended 31 March 1973 were then completed, showing profits of £464,000 on which a dividend of 12.6 per cent was declared. These results were notified to the Stock Exchange on 1 August with an extract from the chairman's report. As regards RFD–GQ, the largest subsidiary, it was stated that while its turnover had increased, it had not reached its profit forecast. The chairman's report, in dealing with the prospects for the current year (1973–74), contained the fateful words, 'I should be surprised if we did not comfortably exceed our last year's forecast of £500,000 pre-tax profits.'

This was offering a hostage to fortune that was almost immediately regretted, for behind the scenes some disquieting facts were emerging. Between the preliminary announcement of the results and the annual general meeting at The Dorchester, London, on 20 September, the auditors' review of the RFD–GQ accounting procedures raised questions about the accuracy of the company's accounts for 1972–73.

These doubts and uncertainties about the Group's financial position could not have come at a more inconvenient time, for negotiations to acquire a specialist textile company in Lancashire had reached a delicate stage and the Group itself was being threatened by a take-over bid from the Avon Rubber Company.

As long ago as November 1968 the Group board had considered a proposal by Perseverance Mill that RFD should acquire a controlling interest in Tranmere Textiles Limited of Blackburn, who had prepared their warps on the beams for many years. (In non-technical language this means twisting the nylon yarn received from the yarn producers and winding it onto long cylinders or warp beams which are then sent to the mill to be woven into fabric.) Tranmere Textiles had been started in 1938 by the father of the present managing director, James Scholfield, who took charge when his father died in 1950. It is a specialised, labour-intensive business staffed almost entirely by women operatives, who usually enter the works straight from school and are trained for two or three years before they are able to handle the full range of yarns processed by the company. Warping is dependent on the skill of the beamer, not the speed of the machine, whereas in weaving it is the speed of the machine that counts and one operator may look after as many as forty looms. Much of the Tranmere production is a continuous process running seven days a week. Although Tranmere work mostly for Perseverance Mill, they do a useful business with other customers. At the time of the take-over negotiations their annual profit was in the region of £125,000.

Tranmere Textiles is an epitome of the Lancashire textile industry, as James Scholfield explained:

> If you are born in it—and the whole area is devoted to it—you live it, it's there—it's a way of life. The textile industry is a skill, based on dexterity. It's a parochial operative force, drawn from very local people, and most of them walk to work. This is good in one sense, but bad if you strike a difficult patch and it affects a whole locality—it's bad in that sense. Whole families work in one mill—Tranmere had one in which the father, his wife, three daughters and a son-in-law all worked here at the mill. You get this in Lancashire. The mill becomes the concern of the whole family. Mind you, as the local saying goes, if you hurt one, the others all limp.

A mill is started by a man who knows everybody by name. They know and call him by his name—they call me Jim here, the older ones, not the young ones. And this is how it is at Perseverance.

Nothing had been done about the proposal to acquire Tranmere Textiles in 1968 because of the Group's current financial position, but the subject came up again at the beginning of 1972, when it was suggested that Tranmere might be acquired by the issue of loan stock in exchange for the Tranmere ordinary shares. The Tranmere board (which included two directors of Perseverance Mill) were sufficiently interested to allow a detailed investigation by the RFD auditors to be put in hand with a view to a formal offer being made.

While this was going on, Miss Irene Burke, the major shareholder in Tranmere and a director of the company, was killed in a motorway accident on 12 July 1972. In the ensuing months this gave rise to considerable anxiety at Perseverance, who were looking to Tranmere for 75 to 80 per cent of their supplies of prepared synthetic yarn for their £500,000 expansion programme of installing a large number of the latest Saurer looms. If the control of Tranmere were to pass into the hands of a rival mill with its own requirements for prepared yarn, Perseverance might find their supplies of warps in jeopardy, which would seriously erode their profitability, because the alternative of installing their own processing plant would entail very heavy capital expenditure. This fear became a real threat when it was learnt in May 1973 that Hollas Textiles were looking into the possibility of acquiring Tranmere.

During the next few months there were lengthy discussions with Hill Samuel & Co Limited, the merchant bankers, about the terms on which an offer might be made for the Tranmere shares.

Before continuing with the history of the Tranmere negotiations it is necessary to go back a few months to trace the development that had taken place with Avon Rubber. Their interest in RFD dated back to the previous March when David Mynors had met an old Imperial Tobacco colleague, Hugh Rogers, who had been deputy chairman and had subsequently retired. He was now part-time chairman of Avon Rubber and he asked Mynors to pass on a message from John Swanborough, the managing director, inviting the chairman and managing director of RFD to meet the directors of Avon Rubber to discuss the possibility of a take-over. This would strengthen Avon's inflatable dinghy and liferaft business, and Rogers added that Avon were in a position to supply RFD with proofed fabric, regardless of any take-over negotiations. In return, Avon Rubber were in the market for woven fabric.

RFD knew that there had been a considerable turnover in their shares in recent months, ending up with large blocks of shares being held by nominees, but Rogers assured Mynors that Avon Rubber had nothing to do with these nominee shares.

This led to a formal meeting between the two sides at a London hotel attended by de Boinville, Mynors and Wylie on the RFD side and Rogers, Swanborough and Fisher, the sales director, for Avon Rubber. The advantages of amalgamation and many aspects of the two businesses were discussed, and further meetings on a managing director level were planned. Afterwards Rogers told de Boinville that if the deal went through, Avon Rubber could provide a factory in South Wales as an alternative to the additional RFD-GQ factory for which a lease was currently being negotiated in Newcastle-upon-Tyne.

At a board meeting on 16 May the RFD directors decided that de Boinville should inform Rogers that the Group were not in favour of being acquired by Avon Rubber on the grounds that unless the take-over bid price were exceedingly generous, the shareholders would benefit to a greater extent by continuing to hold their investments in the RFD Group. Nevertheless, Swanborough and Wylie should explore the areas where the two companies might collaborate to mutual advantage.

A few days later de Boinville was asked by a man named Gordon Hay to meet him for lunch at Chiddingfold. It transpired that he was the managing director of Bodycote International (a Slater Walker company) which was in a similar line of business to Mills Equipment—they were a textile sewing company making webbing—and they had a holding of about 750,000 shares in RFD. Hay wanted to start discussions on how the two companies could collaborate—and possibly amalgamate. De Boinville consulted Hill Samuel, whose advice was that it would not be in the interests of RFD shareholders to make a bid for Bodycote or to be taken over by them. After a meeting between Hill Samuel and Slater Walker, the Group decided to end their negotiations with Hay.

Nothing more happened on this front until the morning of 6 November, when Avon Rubber informed RFD that in the last few days they had acquired substantial blocks of RFD shares and now held

2,648,500 ordinary shares amounting to 23 per cent of the issued ordinary share capital. They now intended to make an offer for the remaining shares. (One of the blocks of RFD shares was the 8 per cent holding by Bodycote, which Hay had sold when his own dealings with RFD came to an end.)

This message was received on the very same day on which a press announcement, as required by the Stock Exchange, was to be issued stating that all the Tranmere preference shareholders and 51.8 per cent of the ordinary shareholders had undertaken to accept the RFD offer to acquire the whole issued capital of Tranmere Textiles on the basis of £2 for each preference share and 29 RFD ordinary shares of 10p each for each Tranmere ordinary share. A further statement that Avon Rubber had requested talks that might lead to their making an offer to acquire all the issued ordinary shares of RFD (of which they already held 23 per cent) was added to the press announcement, which was issued in the afternoon of 6 November.

On 24 November Hill Samuel, on behalf of RFD, made a written offer to the shareholders of Tranmere in which details of the 1973 published profits of £464,000 were repeated. The offer was made unconditional on 17 December, by which time 100 per cent acceptances had been received, and a total of 2,030,290 RFD ordinary shares of 10p each were issued and allotted.

Although there had been no discussion on the point during the negotiations with Tranmere and Avon Rubber, doubts about RFD reaching their profit forecast in the first six months ended 30 September 1973 hung like a dark cloud over the minds of the Group directors. Their worst forebodings were confirmed towards the end of December when work on the delayed half-yearly accounts for the Group to 30 September brought to light an overstatement of at least £135,000 in the published profits of RFD-GQ for the year ended 31 March 1973. Provision should have been made for short deliveries and warranty claims in respect of the sales of a number of gunnery trainers. In computing the profits for the year to 31 March 1973 credit had been taken in full for the sales of these dome trainers, although in some cases they had not—by that date—been delivered and in others it was known that there were substantial short deliveries and pending warranty claims.

Towards the end of December further matters came to light affecting the RFD–GQ accounts for the year ended 31 March 1973—there were serious errors in the valuation of stocks and work in progress. By the middle of January it became apparent that the effect of the various adjustments being carried out might eliminate a substantial part of the reported RFD–GQ profit of £153,000.

A decisive meeting, which lasted all day, was held at the offices of Hill Samuel. The RFD directors reported that the results of RFD–GQ for the year ended 31 March 1973 had been overstated by an estimated £135,000 while those for the half year to 30 September were expected to show a loss, as yet unquantified. Although the other companies had together achieved pre-tax profits of some £192,000, it was expected that the Group as a whole would show a loss. It was agreed that the only proper course was to ask the Stock Exchange for a temporary suspension of listing of the securities of the RFD Group. The application was made on 21 January 1974 at a meeting with the Stock Exchange Council lasting about an hour. The council were very reluctant to accede to the request, but finally agreed. RFD were asked to go back to the Council as soon as they thought the company was on a sound footing again, and to do this as soon as possible. The suspension took effect from the following day and a press statement was issued setting out the reasons.

Alan Wylie was relieved of his executive duties on 29 January 1974, from which date Charles de Boinville and Ted Queening took over responsibility for Group matters and overseas subsidiaries, Gerald Boxall was made responsible for RFD–GQ, and Jeremy Higham for Perseverance and Tranmere.

Two days after the suspension, de Boinville was asked to bring some colleagues to a meeting in the Avon Rubber sales office at Reading. Hugh Rogers, the chairman, bitterly complained about the position they now found themselves in, to which de Boinville could only reply that he was sorry, but it was too bad: 'We couldn't let you know about it any earlier because we didn't know ourselves.' He promised to keep Rogers informed about developments.

Some of the former shareholders of Tranmere Textiles (in particular Keith Burke, who had inherited the majority shareholding from his aunt) took a more belligerent line. A number of meetings took place at Hill Samuel's offices, always with solicitors present on both sides. To begin with they considered suing the individual RFD directors for false representation in their take-over offer; instead they instituted proceedings against the Group on the same grounds claiming recission of the contract to exchange shares, and damages. (Eventually the dispute

All 17 members of the crew of the Fleetwood motor trawler *Irvana* reached the shore safely in three RFD 10-man liferafts when the vessel went on the rocks at Red Bay, Cushenden, County Antrim, Northern Ireland

Five men and their dog. These Danish fishermen and their boxer escaped in a 6-man RFD liferaft when they had to abandon the trawler *E.N. Christiansen* in a North Sea gale in 1972. Half an hour later they were picked up by the German naval vessel *Freiburg*

(*above*) Lifting a casualty in a vertical position is one of many special uses of the versatile Paraguard stretcher made by RFD Mills Equipment. It has been supplied to ambulance and rescue services, fire brigades, the armed forces, airlines, shipping companies and industrial organisations throughout the world; (*below*) a Boeing 727 airliner being lifted by the pneumatic elevators of RFD aircraft recovery equipment after crashing at Fiumicino airport, Rome, in 1978. This equipment is now available at many airports throughout the world

Another rescue from disaster: air-lift cushions manufactured by the RFD subsidiary, MFC Survival Ltd, raising an overturned 2,000-gallon tanker so that the driver of the Austin Princess crushed beneath it could be released and the car removed. In spite of the bodywork being flattened, Andrew Lodge sustained only a fractured collar bone and minor injuries. The rescue and recovery team operated by D.G. McAlister of Aldershot, working under the direction of the fire service, inserted a MFC heavy-lift three-compartment air cushion unit under the tanker and inflated it with compressed air from their air van

Infant air travellers with scaled-down versions of the latest adult RFD life-jacket that has been sold in tens of thousands since its introduction in 1975

was settled by the payment of compensation and the claims against the Group were dropped.)

RFD's first step, recommended by both Hill Samuel and the Stock Exchange Council, was to call in a firm of independent accountants to go through the whole organisation and report. This task was undertaken by Peat, Marwick, Mitchell & Company, working jointly with Andw W. Barr & Co, the RFD auditors.

By the end of February it was clear to the accountants that no reliable figures were obtainable for RFD–GQ for the six months to September 1973. On 25 March revised instructions were sent to them to abandon the investigation of the accounts to 30 September; instead, they were to prepare a joint report on the overstatement of the profits in the RFD–GQ accounts to 31 March 1973 and on the steps being taken to remedy any deficiencies in the accounting system. This report was to be included in the Group report and accounts for the year ended 31 March 1974, and this was made a condition for the re-listing of the shares on the Stock Exchange.

All this was disclosed in a circular to the shareholders issued on 27 March, which added that the rest of the Group had been trading profitably and was fully up to budget, but as a result of the problems of RFD–GQ and the effects of the energy crisis, it now appeared probable that the Group's trading results for the present financial year would show an overall loss.

As the group managing director and chairman of the RFD–GQ subsidiary, Alan Wylie was obviously in a vulnerable position, and the relinquishment of his executive duties at the end of January was followed by the termination of his service agreement as from 31 March. For the time being the duties of the group managing director were jointly assumed by de Boinville in a non-executive capacity and by Queening as an executive.

Without a chairman, RFD–GQ now became the sole responsibility of the new managing director, Gerald Boxall, who had joined the Group as an additional director in November and had a month's induction period before taking up his duties. In his early thirties, Boxall had tremendous drive coupled with great courage and management expertise which combined to make him the ideal trouble-shooter. In talks with David Mynors, who had been put on the RFD–GQ board in November 1973, it was agreed that his first priority was to extricate the company from the stranglehold of fixed price contracts that were taking the profit out of much of their work. The prices in these contracts did not take into account the severe cost inflation experienced by RFD–GQ in common with British industry generally. Indeed, parachutes were being sold for less than it cost to make them. In the absence of any figures on which to calculate individual price increases, Boxall simply added a flat percentage increase across the board. Fortunately the products were so good that customers accepted this rough-and-ready treatment with little effect on sales.

Gerald Boxall set about renegotiating the contracts with ruthless determination. Charles de Boinville recalls the day when he went with him to the Ministry of Defence.:

> On the way I told Boxall we would support anything he did, even though it might put us out of business. When we saw the Assistant Permanent Secretary, Boxall said, 'I'm going to tear up these contracts' —and he did. The Ministry could do nothing about it and eventually had to accept the situation. It was a very brave thing to do, but we were there, with him, and we let him loose.

On the inflatables side the position was not quite so bad. There were a certain number of fixed price contracts, particularly in Scandinavia, and Boxall adopted the same sort of tough tactics there. De Boinville added:

> I warned the board that we might have a bomb blow up in our faces if any of our customers sued us for breach of contract, but none of them did. We were taking a considerable chance, but eventually it put RFD–GQ back as quite a decent profit earner.

When Boxall had arrived on the scene there was something like a two-year order book for some of the products. Putting up the prices slashed the order book significantly—but the cash started to come in and the company was making a profit. By getting the prices right Boxall gave RFD–GQ—and indeed the Group—the essential breathing space to set the whole business to rights.

In between leaving Delanair (a subsidiary of Lindustries) and joining RFD, Gerald Boxall had helped to organise the Round-Britain yacht race, which was due to take place in June–July 1974, and he himself had teamed up with the famous Robin Knox-Johnson in entering a catamaran. This inevitably gave rise to a critical situation. From the point of view of RFD everything depended on the Group putting its house in order—and being seen to be doing so—before the annual general meeting in August. In the face of opposition from some members of the board, Charles de Boinville, as chairman, gave Boxall permission to fulfil his commitments to the race organisers and his team-mate, even though it meant his being away—and what is more, at sea—during those four or five critical weeks. But de Boinville did not have any regrets:

> He was a great sailor, and he had made all the arrangements before he joined us, so I let him go. I had great pleasure in following his progress in the race, which they won. And that indirectly did RFD a lot of good.

Boxall transformed the position of RFD–GQ, not only by renegotiating many of the fixed price contracts and ensuring that all orders taken from the beginning of January were at realistic prices (usually with a price-adjustment clause) but also by a fundamental reorganisation of the company. He replaced the central control of the five divisions (which in effect were treated as little more than departments) by the appointment of a director/general manager for each division and making him responsible and accountable for its profitability and for all functions except finance.

The accounts for the year ended 31 March 1974 were published on 29 July and they revealed the full extent of that disastrous year for the first time. The Group loss amounted to £350,281 which, taken in conjunction with the expectation of a profit 'comfortably exceeding £500,000' forecast by the chairman at the previous annual general meeting, meant an adverse turn-round in the Group's affairs of some £850,000. Of this total, £181,000 was accounted for by the overstatement of profits in the previous year, but the major factor was the loss by RFD–GQ of £756,076. On the credit side, the profits of the other companies in the Group had risen from £31,525 in 1972–73 to £405,759.

The publication of the accounts produced an immediate response from Avon Rubber, who were smarting under the shock of seeing their RFD shares, which had just been re-listed on the Stock Exchange and for which they had paid 33p, drop to a mere 3p. (Actually they changed hands at 9½p on the day of the annual general meeting and never looked back afterwards.) What amounted to almost a command was issued to de Boinville to attend a meeting at the Melksham headquarters of Avon Rubber.

This meeting was followed later by demands from Avon Rubber for strong representation on the RFD board. In the end it was agreed that they should have two places on the board with an alternate who could attend meetings if one of the other directors could not be present.

The directors nominated by Avon Rubber and elected following the annual general meeting on 20 August were John Swanborough, the managing director, and Alan Craig, with Peter Giles as an alternate. The last two had recently set up as Craig Giles, management consultants, operating from a flat in Regent's Park. In view of the important position Alan Craig was to hold in the Group, it is worth looking at his career up to that point. In his own words:

> I went from Newcastle University to Manchester Business School, where I did a two-year course. In 1970 I left Manchester and went to Slater Walker, where I was on the industrial side looking after their industrial interests. I was then 25. At the beginning of 1974 I left Slater Walker to join Peter Giles—a New Zealander by birth—and we did everything to do with business. We got the cash flow!
>
> In July, through a third party, I went down to see John Swanborough, the managing director of Avon, and asked him what they proposed to do about their investment in RFD. I suggested they should use us as consultants, to see what was going on. The upshot was that in a few weeks' time we found ourselves on the RFD board with Swanborough.

In October 1974 Craig and Giles were invited to become acting joint chief executives of the Group. This was a temperary measure while the board made up its mind about appointing a group managing director. By February 1975 they had considered all the alternatives and came down in favour of Alan Craig, who accepted the post. On Craig's appointment as full-time group managing director, Peter Giles was made a non-executive director.

As the non-executive chairman of the Group, Charles de Boinville had borne the brunt of the traumatic period since Wylie's departure left the Group without a managing director, notwithstanding the help he received from Mynors, now deputy chairman and Queening, the finance director. His health had inevitably been affected—his doctor had warned him that his blood pressure was much too high for someone who had had a heart attack, and that he should not go on—so shortly after the annual general meeting he wisely resigned. As David Mynors, who succeeded him, reminded the shareholders at the next annual general meeting, several of the basic decisions which had led to the recovery of the Group were taken while de Boinville was still chairman.

In the circumstances it was a pity that his departure was preceded by an acrimonious exchange with the Avon Rubber board. They demanded not only his resignation but that of David Mynors as well. De Boinville told Rogers, the Avon Rubber chairman, that in view of the state of his health he was going to resign anyway, but he resisted very strongly any suggestion of Mynors going too. The RFD board endorsed his attitude by appointing Mynors chairman in his place.

In his final statement to the shareholders in the report and accounts for the year ended 31 March 1974 Charles de Boinville was understandably careful to restrict his forecast for the prospects of the Group to the guarded comment 'there are reasonable grounds for hoping that the Group as a whole will at least break even in the current financial year'. In fact they turned a loss of £350,000 into a resounding record profit of £1,431,000, on which a final dividend of 8.789 per cent was paid.

This remarkable recovery, which substantially rehabilitated the Group in the eyes of the City and the markets in which it operated, was largely due to Gerald Boxall's initial action in raising the prices of the Group's products to a realistic level. Great credit was also due to the transformation of its financial management by Ted Queening, who introduced all the controls and information procedures that had been so sadly lacking in the past. And as joint chief executives in the second half of the year, Alan Craig and Peter Giles were able to identify what was happening and establish the confidence to persevere. As Peter Giles said later: 'We could see that even if our cash flow was still negative and things were pretty black, things were moving in the right direction and that the action taken by Gerald was the right action.'

It was in RFD–GQ, of course, that the biggest part of the recovery was made—indeed needed to be made, for there had never been anything wrong with the other companies and they continued to be profitable throughout the crisis. The decentralisation begun by Boxall with a director/general manager in charge of each of the five divisions was extended so that each division acted as a separate profit centre with its own financial manager. The process was completed with effect from 1 April 1975 when the Group board transferred the assets and activities of each trading division of RFD–GQ into separate subsidiary companies —RFD Inflatables Ltd, GQ Parachutes Ltd, RFD Systems Engineering Ltd and RFD Mills Equipment Ltd. The ill-fated RFD–GQ Ltd ceased to operate as a trading subsidiary. As David Mynors put it in his statement accompanying the 1975 accounts:

The more effective management, tighter control of operating methods and more realistic commercial policies resulted in RFD–GQ turning in a record performance from the point of view of sales, trading profit and return on capital. The achievement was due to great efforts on the part of the employees of all grades in circumstances which at times were most unsettling and demonstrates what can be done under proper leadership if people pull together.

That leadership, of course, had come in the first place from Gerald Boxall, the RFD–GQ managing director, and it was a great loss to the Group when, four days before the 1975 annual general meeting, he handed in his resignation. He had fulfilled to perfection his role as trouble-shooter, and as de Boinville remarked later: 'He played a significant part in achieving the recovery of RFD–GQ at a much quicker rate than we had expected.'

Three weeks earlier John Swanborough had resigned from the RFD board as a nominee of the Avon Rubber Company as a consequence of his resignation from Avon, who were now in a bad trading position themselves. In December they disposed of their holding in RFD to institutions and the Group thereby regained its independence, with its largest shareholder (Imperial Tobacco Pension Fund) holding only 6 per cent of the equity.

In the circumstances it came as no surprise when the auditors, Andw W. Barr & Company, resigned in October 1975 and the firm of Touche Ross & Company were appointed in their stead.

In retrospect the crisis can be seen as a hiccup—albeit amounting to almost a paroxysm—in the steady growth and progress of the RFD Group over the years. It needs to be emphasised that its cause was confined to RFD–GQ, the major manufacturing subsidiary. The other manufacturing subsidiary, Perseverance Mill, was unaffected, and the whole Group—including the divisions within RFD–GQ—continued throughout to turn out first-class products which were in constant demand.

The then members of the Group board cannot escape their share of responsibility. They were at fault in not insisting on being provided by the managers with the up-to-date management information required to monitor the performance of RFD–GQ until it was almost too late. As it was, the plunge from an estimated profit of £500,000 to a loss of £350,000 in the space of twelve months opened up an abyss from which the Group was only saved in the nick of time.

Later events showed that the recovery in the Group's fortunes in 1974–75 was no mere flash in the pan. After the record profit of £1,431,000 in that year, the Group continued to surge forward with an increase of 47 per cent in 1975–76 to £2,103,000, followed by a further increase of 56 per cent to £3,283,000 in 1976–77.

Before the crisis the profit had only once topped £500,000 (in 1967–68 the figure was £505,642).

CHAPTER TWELVE

SIXTY YEARS ON

After wrestling with the complexities of the financial crisis in the last chapter, it is refreshing to turn once more to the real heart of the Group —the products that kept the flag flying high throughout the darkest days—and to see how they are faring in this sixtieth year of RFD history.

When Inflation Saves Lives

Taking RFD Inflatables first, a major success was achieved in 1969–70 with orders to supply 32-seater circular liferafts for the Boeing 747s and DC-10s going into service on the airlines (with one exception) operating these aircraft outside the United States. Liferafts of this type are nowadays carried by most European airlines. At the other end of the scale, RFD continue to supply single-seat liferafts for fighter aircraft of the RAF and many other air forces. In between, there are 10-seater and 18-seater liferafts for intermediate-size aircraft, and the Seafly liferaft for light aeroplanes which can take up to six people and has a built-in canopy with four observation posts. (The Seafly is remarkably compact —together with full emergency equipment, it is carried in a hand valise weighing only 10 kilos.)

With models to carry 4, 6, 8, 10, 12, 15, 20 and 25 people, the range of RFD marine liferafts provides for every class of ship or boat. By 1979 more than 500,000 were currently in service throughout the world with shipping lines, ferries (including hovercraft), fishing and merchant vessels, yachts and leisure craft, and were standard equipment in a score of navies. Indeed, it was the Brazilian Navy in 1971 that brought in the largest single export order in the company's history to date—700,000 dollars-worth of 15-man liferafts with full emergency packs and marine life-jackets for re-equipping the navy with inflatable survival equipment. What made this order particularly gratifying was that it was obtained in the face of competitive tenders by a dozen manufacturers in the United States, Europe and the United Kingdom.

At the Southampton Boat Show in 1976 RFD introduced the Surviva 6-man liferaft for yachtsmen—the first liferaft to be produced by high-frequency electronic bonding of the seams. The Surviva was an immediate success, and was followed at the same boat show in 1978 by the 4-man Seasava, using the same manufacturing technique. By that time some 4,000 Survivas had been delivered.

The first rescue by Seasava was a dramatic one. In July 1979 Kenneth Kerr attempted to row across the Atlantic single-handed in his 13ft *Bass Conqueror* but capsized in violent seas 700 miles off the Canadian coast. He took to the 4-man Seasava and was located with the aid of his pocket-sized Locat survival radio transmitter. Some 30 hours later a Royal Canadian Air Force aircraft dropped a large liferaft 50 yards away and he rowed to it with the paddle provided in the Seasava, which Kerr reported had been remarkably stable in 50ft seas. (Four months later the barnacle-covered *Bass Conqueror* drifted ashore on the north coast of Ireland.)

Similar rescues by dropping a liferaft into the sea from an aircraft are done with the Lindholme gear, described earlier. The Mark 4 version, with containers made of glass fibre instead of compressed card, is in use with Nimrod aircraft of RAF Strike Command and can be dropped at anything between 125 and 250 knots.

The number of lives saved by RFD liferafts (many incidents, of course, go unrecorded) is estimated to be in excess of 20,000—many of them in conditions of extreme severity of weather and endurance, the reports coming from all parts of the world.

In 1967 RFD announced the introduction of a 20-man liferaft for use in conjunction with submarines. Nicknamed Project Egg (on account of the shape of its container) it had been inherited from Elliott Equipment when that company was acquired by RFD in 1963, and in the intervening years had been developed in conjunction with the RFD licensees, Hanseatische Retungsgeraete Fabrik GmbH of Hamburg and Bremen. The liferaft with full emergency pack and equipment bag was packed in a glass fibre container which had 260lb buoyancy and was designed to resist water pressure at a depth in excess of 200ft. In the event of a disaster the container, which was connected to the submarine housing by a painter, was released and the operating head was tripped by a cable. But instead of inflating the liferaft immediately, the operating head was pressed down by a stop-button until it was released as the water pressure decreased at about 20ft below the surface. The hydrostatic head was then triggered off and the liferaft started to inflate, breaking out of the container as it bobbed to the surface, there to await the arrival of survivors from the submarine. Project Egg was taken up by the German and Norwegian navies, but is no longer marketed by RFD.

In the same year, 1967, the retirement of Mrs Grace Dobson ('Dobby'), the production manageress, received official acknowledgement by the award of the British Empire Medal for her services to export and management—an event that gave great pleasure and satisfaction throughout the Group. During the forty-five years of the company's history—and for several years previously as one of Reginald Dagnall's earliest employees at Airships Limited—she had been in charge of countless women and girls working in the RFD factories and had built up an extraordinary facility in gaining their confidence and co-operation. This had been particularly valuable during the war, when (in Anton Bik's words) 'the company was seen through the most difficult times by the hard work of the women employees. Much of the work was done on the floor, sewing balloon fabric, and they worked long hours, often to the point of exhaustion.' And Dr Mercer, the company doctor, added, 'She knew all about the work, and was marvellous in managing the women. She was like a mother to them.'

The RNLI inshore rescue lifeboat made by RFD (of which more than 100 are in use around the coast) is a variant of the Z-boat Type PB16 which is also used for airport crash rescue, oil and diving operations, expeditions and water ski-ing. The company received widespread publicity in 1972 when RFD PB16 Z-boats were used by the trans-British Columbia expedition, led by Captain Sir Ranulph Twistleton-Wikeham-Fiennes. The expedition consisted of a team of soldiers, an RNLI rescue man and photographers from the *Observer* newspaper and the BBC. The 2,300-mile journey, which had never been done before, included shooting some of the most dangerous rapids in the world, and the RFD boats featured prominently in the thrilling film that was shown twice on BBC 2.

RFD inflatables were also chosen for the Colombian Amazonas Expedition in 1977, which aimed to carry out a scientific study of the area to develop its natural resources without damaging the environment. Four teams of British and Colombian scientists operated for several months from a base camp in the heart of the rain forest and were deployed for distances up to 250 miles along the river by seven RFD Z-boats—four PB16s which carried up to eight people with light equipment and three 380s for 3-man crews engaged on monitoring and survey work. RFD type-80 life-jackets were worn on all river trips, but none had to be used in anger.

With experience gained from the Z-boats, RFD have produced a DoT-approved 12ft 6in Class C workboat which has the advantage of doing away with the heavy davit on the stern of fishing vessels, required for the usual rigid workboat. It is powered by a DoT-approved $9\frac{1}{2}$hp outboard motor.

Over the years RFD Inflatables have developed life-jackets—marine and aircraft—to a very high standard of safety and convenience. They are designed to be self-righting, so that even an unconscious person is held at the correct flotation angle, and the shape ensures not only proper head support (face upwards and the head well clear of the water) but also that the body is turned to face the oncoming sea and waves— an essential requirement for survival. With one exception they can be inflated instantaneously by pulling the toggle of a CO_2 bottle attached to the jacket, and can be topped up by mouth. They carry a whistle and an optional water-activated battery light to help rescuers spot survivors at night, while in daytime the bright yellow colour of the fabric shows up their position.

The exception is the life-jacket designed to be worn inflated or partly inflated at all times, for which mouth inflation is sufficient. An alternative life-jacket for constant wear afloat is enclosed (deflated) in a halter round the neck and can be immediately inflated by activating the gas bottle, which inflates the jacket by bursting through the halter. Another life-jacket, which was primarily designed for commercial use and is now in service with many navies around the world, has been modified for use by leisure sailors. It differs from other models in being carried in a pouch worn around the waist, from where it can be quickly placed round the neck and inflated by gas bottle in an emergency. The Mark 3 model of this life-jacket was ordered by Trinity House for their twenty pilots at Milford Haven, Britain's leading oil refinery port, after one of them was drowned while disembarking from a tanker off St Ann's Head. They asked RFD to give a demonstration and the order was placed immediately.

RFD marine life-jackets received a public commendation in 1962 when the magazine *Which?* chose the forerunner of the present Aquasport model as the 'best buy' among the twenty-six different models they tested. From a short list of four, it was the only one that had none of the disadvantages possessed by the other three.

The most popular aircraft life-jacket in the RFD range—tens of thousands have been sold to airlines all over the world—is a model which is equally suitable for adults and for children from four years old upwards. For younger children—infants weighing up to 35lb—there is a special life-jacket which has all the attributes of the larger model, together with a lifeline for an adult to hold. The latest infant life-jacket was exhibited for the first time at the 1979 Paris Air Show. All these RFD aircraft life-jackets are instantaneously inflated by jerking the CO_2 gas bottle toggle, and have automatic sea lights. They have full Civil Aviation Authority approval.

As every hunger-striker knows, drinking water is more important for survival than food. With the great increase in the number of people at risk from this danger brought about by the availability of inflatable liferafts, the Government gave RFD a design contract for a solar still. The device consists of a cone and buoyancy chamber which can be inflated and moored alongside a liferaft to produce drinking water by the effect of evaporation and condensation under solar heating. It works best of course when exposed to the sun, but will continue to produce drinkable water even in overcast weather. At peak performance it produces 175cc an hour. Sea water, contaminated water or urine is placed in the base chamber sump—the product is the same, pure drinking water. The RFD solar still is in service with the RAF and has CAA approval for use by airlines. It is also in demand for sea and land expeditions.

Another application of the inflatable concept developed by RFD is the Numax hut, which is made in two sizes and has countless uses, both for emergencies and for special purposes. It can be erected manually in about 45 minutes, by means of an electric blower in about 4 minutes, and by a compressed air cylinder in 3 minutes.

Inflatable escape slides continue to be in demand and a programme of development of special slides for the Concorde was completed in 1973, most of the cost being met by Government funds. An ingenious feature was that three of the six slides were instantly convertible into liferafts. A separate 36-seater liferaft was also carried. The overall specification required the full complement of passengers to be able to leave the aircraft within 90 seconds of landing, using only half the equipment, so the inflation and operation of the slides had to be as automatic and rapid as possible. When the time came for the Concorde to go into service in 1976, RFD bought a return ticket for the inaugural flight to Bahrain and raffled it among the employees at Godalming, Woking, Waterloo-ville and Belfast. The winner was Mrs Evelyn Patton of Belfast, who had a 'fantastic' trip—the farthest she had ever been before was on a boat to Scotland.

The Soviet Union quickly recognised the value of the escape slide and placed a contract through their foreign trade organisation for the RFD equipment for their Ilyushin 62 MK airliner. (Through the USSR trade delegation in London, RFD had previously supplied liferafts and life-jackets to Aeroflot.) The inflatable escape slide lends itself to various applications apart from aircraft, and prototypes for various purposes are continually being evaluated.

For some of these prototypes the slab material developed during the war for making decoy tanks and military vehicles was used to stiffen the structure. As the reader may recall, this comprised two layers of fabric linked together by tie threads which also kept them apart. It occurred to someone that this slab material would solve the problem of making a really stable inflation bag for pneumatic lifting gear used for rapidly removing crashed aircraft from runways. The earlier design produced by Reginald Dagnall during the war had cylindrical bags which tended to become circular when they were inflated—as Fred Scott remarked, 'it had built-in instability'. The American weavers obliged by weaving material in greater depth (the two layers of fabric are linked together in the weaving process), experiments having shown that the optimum distance between the layers was 9in.

A new system of lifting equipment was therefore introduced by RFD in 1969, capable of lifting aircraft weighing up to 350 tons—powerful enough to handle Jumbo jets. A live demonstration at Orly airport in the autumn of 1970 led to several firm orders being received, as well as many enquiries. Since then, with the recommendation of the International Civil Aviation Organisation, RFD aircraft recovery equipment has been made available at airports all over the world including Heathrow, Orly, Stuttgart, Geneva, Vienna and Athens; Tripoli, Kuwait, Jedda, Rijadh and Dahahran; Freetown, Lusaka, Johannesburg, Bombay, Singapore and Manila; and Kennedy airport in the United States. The equipment has also been supplied to the French Air Force.

The complete aircraft-recovery system comprises a set of pneumatic elevators (rectangular 25–40 lb inflation bags built up in series according to the lift required), air compressors and hoses operating through consoles to ensure that the correct pressure is applied to the elevators, Dragonjack inflatable tracks, a movement winch and anchor plates, and a Numax hut which can be used as a first-aid post for casualties from the crashed aircraft and for storage during the operation. The pneumatic elevators enable the fuselage of the aircraft to be lifted sufficiently for the undercarriage to be repaired or lowered, or for the aircraft to be towed away on inflated tracks—a particularly useful facility if the aircraft is blocking a runway.

Among the airports where aircraft have been recovered and removed are Heathrow (Douglas DC8), Gerona (BAC 1–11), Corfu (BAC 1–11), Athens (Boeing 747 cargo), Kano (Fokker F28) and Vienna (Tupolev 134 and Boeing 707). In all cases the recovery equipment reduced the possibility of secondary damage to the aircraft while it was being recovered, thereby enabling it to be brought back into operational service quickly. The incident at Kano involved extricating the Fokker F28 from a mudhole into which it had sunk after overshooting the runway and moving it two miles to within half a mile of the control tower. The distance was too great for the use of inflatable tracks, so the aircraft—with the pneumatic elevators *in situ*—was moved by the UBM Engineering Company's system of a special hover platform.

In a different scene, pneumatic elevators supplied by RFD were found to be extremely useful in controlling the lifting and lowering of a gas pipeline 550ft long, 54in in diameter and weighing 140 tons.

Pneumatic elevators for different purposes are made by a small company, MFC Survival Limited, of Tonypandy, that had been a sales and servicing agent of RFD for many years before it was acquired in 1978. The MFC air-lift unit was developed originally for the fire service and is used mainly for rescuing people who are trapped in road accidents, collapsed buildings, tunnels and trenches, where conventional jacking systems are difficult or impossible to employ. Another MFC product is a reincarnation of the 'Camel' salvage pontoon made by the Airships Limited company managed by Reginald Dagnall in the First World War. The 36in diameter underwater 'Aquasphere' has a surface lift capacity of 900lb and can lift 500lb at a depth of 80ft. A larger model of 48in diameter lifts 1,200lb at depth and can be used singly or in multiples of four. MFC also make spherical pneumatic bags for lifting heavy road vehicles that have overturned. A series of three bags will lift a large tanker without damaging it. MFC lifting gear is widely used in Britain and the United States.

Yet another subsidiary company, RFD Holland, has entered the pneumatic lifting business with a cylindrical bag measuring 2.5 metres by a metre which has an individual lifting capacity of 3.5 tons. With variations in size and number of cylinders, lifts up to 150 tons are obtainable. These lifting cylinders are mainly intended for underwater pipeline operations, where an easy method of bringing pipes to the surface is of great benefit. They are also fitted (deflated) on each side of the harbour workboats in the Damen shipyards in Holland, ready for instant inflation in an emergency to prevent the boat from sinking.

In addition to the acquisition of MFC Survival, RFD added to its inflatable activities early in 1978 by taking a 55 per cent interest in Res-Q-Raft, the inflatable raft business built up by the Patten family at Lake Worth, Florida, and re-naming it RFD–Patten Inc. This was not RFD's first entry into the American market. In 1962 the Group had taken a 50 per cent interest in an American associate, RFD Inc, with the aim of developing the sales of liferafts. Tests were carried out by the US Coastguards, including ballasting a liferaft to capacity and mooring it out in Chesapeake Bay in mid-winter. After thirty days the canopy was caked with ice but the liferaft was still afloat with the buoyancy chamber as retentive as ever. In another test four liferafts were dropped 140ft from a helicopter in San Francisco Bay, all four inflating exactly as required. In a climatic test ten men jumped into water at 34°F, swam to a liferaft, and stayed in it for five days, warmed by body heat only. Although the company was given initial design approval by the US authorities, it was decided to close it down in 1969 and repatriate the profits and investment.

RFD had been the first company to receive approval for supplying inflatable liferafts for shipping in 1954. Twenty-five years later, as this book went to press, RFD Inflatables showed themselves still to the fore by developing a new 84-man survival unit designed in conjunction with Boeing Marine Systems for use in their Jetfoil high-speed passenger craft operating between London and the Continent and Liverpool/Eire. The unit comprises two 42-man liferafts packed in a single glass-fibre container, and each Jetfoil will carry eight 42-man liferafts to provide for the 294 passengers on board plus the crew. The same method was employed in a new 84-man inflatable slide evacuation system that was being developed for conventional ferries with the support and encouragement of the marine safety division of the Board of Trade. Three new ferries being constructed for Townsend Thoresen were likely to be the first to use the new survival and evacuation system.

Since the days when Reginald Dagnall pioneered the inflatable dinghy between the wars, all the patents have run out and today the manufacture of liferafts has become a worldwide industry in which many of the firms engaged in it at home and abroad employ sophisticated methods of quantity production. Nevertheless RFD still contrive to offer an exceptionally wide range of liferafts including standardised models made in competition with the products of companies geared to their mass manufacture. The future of RFD Inflatables could well lie in concentrating on their forte of making high-quality liferafts for special purposes, coupled with the development of further applications of the inflatable technique.

From Start to Finish

Although some progress had been made in the 1960s in replacing the elderly looms at Perseverance Mill with new machinery, much remained to be done. In 1970 agreement was reached in principle with the Industrial Reorganisation Corporation for a loan of up to £500,000 to be advanced to the Group for this purpose, repayable in seven years and carrying an interest rate of 10 per cent per annum. A first tranche of £250,000 was drawn in 1971 and orders were placed for Saurer multi-purpose looms capable of weaving synthetics, cottons and mixtures. The installation of these looms inevitably caused some disruption in the output of the mill in the latter part of 1971 and the spring of 1972. Nevertheless, the prospects were so improved by the new plant that it was decided that the balance of £250,000 to complete the programme was not required from Government sources.

By the middle of 1973 the textile dyeing and finishing section at Godalming (originally set up for the abortive textile printing business started after the war) had been transferred to Padiham, where additional dyeing and finishing equipment was installed in 1974. The purpose was to give Perseverance greater control of the major product lines (typewriter and computer ribbons) and enable it to provide its customers with better quality and service in some of its highly specialised textile products .There was a financial angle too. 'We were sending work to outside finishers,' said Jeremy Higham, 'and paying for it, so it made sense that we should do our own finishing.' The new section at Padiham began to trade as Albion Dyers and Finishers, but not yet as a separate company, and was immediately profitable. Almost from the first, Albion began commission dyeing and finishing for other firms in the textile industry.

The point was made in the last chapter that Perseverance Mill was not in any way responsible for the appalling loss of £350,000 sustained by the RFD Group in the year ended 31 March 1974. As the chairman put it at the annual general meeting:

> I have had to make some disappointing comments up to this point in my statement, but I am now happy to tell you that on the bright side of your Group's activities in the UK is the very satisfactory performance of the Perseverance Mill Company Limited, where despite the effects of the three-day week the profit forecast was exceeded and the actual profit substantially increased over the previous year.

After achieving record turnover and profits in the first part of 1975, Perseverance were hit by the general slump in textiles, but although weaving had to be cut back for several months, full-time working was resumed by the end of the year. Tranmere were affected in the same way, benefiting from the recovery at Perseverance, which normally took about half its capacity, and holding its own with the outside customers who took the rest, in spite of having to contend with severe price-cutting by competitors.

In the reorganisation of the Group that took place on 1 April 1978 the new Specialist Textile Division brought together Perseverance Mill, Tranmere Textiles and Albion Dyers and Finishers (which now became a separate company instead of being merely a trading activity of Perseverance Mill.) Jeremy Higham, a Group executive director, was appointed divisional chief executive.

In the Specialist Textile Division the Group's textile interests are now solidly vertical between the yarn producer and the fabric user. The laboratory at Perseverance provides a technical service for the warping, weaving, finishing and other operations carried out by the three companies in the division. There is also a lot of liaison on technical matters with the other Group companies. The Group has recently shown its faith in the division by sanctioning a major programme of re-equipment at Perseverance Mill to be spread over several years, the first stage being the purchase of a number of Japanese water-jet looms at a cost of £600,000.

Parachutes for all Seasons

In the rearrangement of RFD subsidiary companies into product groups in 1976, the Military Software group comprised GQ Parachutes and its Australian off-shoot, Parachutes Pty, RFD Systems Engineering and Mills Equipment. Parachutes Pty had been started back in 1963 by GQ (who had the majority interest) in conjunction with their old rivals, Irving Air Chute of Great Britain, in order to operate long-term manufacturing licences from both companies. Two years later the association was extended to the Pioneer Parachute Company of the United States. In 1973–74 GQ bought out the Irving minority interest while continuing to manufacture and distribute their parachutes. In recent years it has been found more economical for Parachutes Pty to supply the Australian market with parachutes made at Godalming.

When the product groups were made into divisions two years later, the companies in Military Software were made the Special Products Division, in which they were joined by Mayday Equipment (a small company that had been acquired at Bridgend, South Wales, making webbing equipment, protective clothing for the Army and various kinds of flare parachutes) and an infant plastics unit recently formed by GQ—also at Bridgend. When the acquisition of Mayday Equipment was completed, their parachute business was transferred to GQ. Graham Davis, managing director of GQ Parachutes, was made divisional chief executive.

The range of GQ parachutes covers parachutes for aircrew escape (including those used with ejection seats), main and reserve military man-dropping parachutes for airborne forces, sports parachutes, aircraft brake parachutes, cargo-dropping assemblies, low-dropping parachute systems and weapon-delivery systems. GQ is the only British-owned parachute company approved by the Ministry of Defence for design, production and inspection to the highest standards.

In spite of GQ's success in designing and supplying escape systems for the ejection seats used by Folland, Saab and the Canadian Air Force (described in an earlier chapter), their parachutes were not specified for the widely used Martin-Baker ejection seat. This went on until 1973, when Arthur Harrison at last managed to get an interview with Sir James Martin. The meeting happened to coincide with an incident in which the Irving parachute used by Martin-Baker was damaged during a high-speed ejection test. Sir James decided the time had come to evaluate GQ's capabilities, and as a result every Martin-Baker Mark 10 ejection seat is now fitted with the GQ Aeroconical parachute, which is in service in twenty-four aircraft types all over the world, including the United States. The aircraft concerned include the British–German–Italian Tornado, the McDonnell Douglas F-18, the Italian Macchi, the RAF Hawk, and the Mig 19s used by the Pakistan Air Force (who have reported the saving of eleven lives to date).

The keen interest in the Martin-Baker ejection seat shown in the United States was the main reason for RFD purchasing the Security Parachute Company near Oakland, California, in 1978, which was re-named GQ–Security Parachutes Inc, and made a part of the Special Products Division. Being able to supply GQ Aeroconical parachutes for Martin-Baker ejection seats from an American factory would forestall the otherwise inevitable objection to a British-made parachute being used by the American Forces. The company is one of the best-known manufacturers of sporting parachutes in the United States and is an approved supplier of military parachutes. In a broader context, David Mynors looked on this acquisition (coupled with that of RFD–Patten, the inflatables concern) as something more than a direct benefit to the Group. In his chairman's statement in the 1978 report and accounts he commented: 'I confidently expect that exposure to the United States at first hand will have a significantly invigorating influence on our management. These two purchases, therefore, constitute an important psychological milestone in the Group's history.'

For the many aircraft not fitted with ejection seats, GQ supply a back-type parachute which is particularly suitable for use in helicopters and gliders where space is restricted.

Parachutes for airborne forces are no longer the relatively simple devices they were when Raymond Quilter produced the Statichute during the war. Today they have to be designed to cope with various types of operations, from the straightforward drop by troops of limited experience from aircraft flying at 100–200 knots to drops by special forces from a great height with the opening of the parachute delayed automatically until the parachutist reaches a pre-determined altitude. In 1967 the highly manoeuvrable tactical assault parachute was introduced for operations in restricted drop-zones at high and low altitudes, while the 22ft steerable parachute is the only static-line parachute approved by the British Government for 'rear-exiting' from the C-130 Hercules.

GQ do not confine themselves to supplying parachutes for airborne forces. They offer a complete development package—the organisation of training facilities, testing, packing and maintenance.

For many years British parachutists regarded Americans as rather 'chicken' for insisting on carrying a reserve parachute in case the main canopy failed to open, but in about 1960 they at last realised that it made sense and would save quite a few lives. Today GQ make a 17ft reserve parachute with a standard canopy and a steerable model with a conical-shaped canopy with two netted nylon lower panels.

An entirely new type of parachute for cargo-carrying was introduced in the early 1970s in which the traditional fabric was replaced by polypropylene material. Instead of varying the size of the whole canopy to suit the load, the new parachute was of modular construction and specific load requirements were met by selecting sufficient crown and wing sections (which were square in shape) and tying them together with polypropylene cords.

Sport parachute design has come a long way since the blank-gore type was developed in the 1950s. The Pathfinder was introduced in 1972–73 and immediately found favour with clubs and as an advertising device. The latest type is the GQ Unit ram-air sports parachute.

The range of aircraft brake parachutes—also introduced in the 1950s—has been expanded to cover most types of aircraft.

The design and development of parachutes are the responsibility of Arthur Harrison, the technical director of Knaphill, who maintains close contact with important customers at home and abroad (in the last twenty years he has made at least fifty trips to Sweden alone). New parachutes are tested first in dummy drops from observation balloons at the Army depot at Hankley Common near Aldershot. The next step is to test them in 'live' drops at the Aircraft and Armament Experimental Establishment at Boscombe Down on Salisbury Plain, with which GQ have always had a very close relationship. Sports parachutes are tested a few miles away at Netheravon. About 50 per cent of new parachute designs are PV (private ventures), the rest being Government development contracts.

Over the years GQ have developed webbing restraint harness that is now used by aircrew in the RAF, the Royal Navy, and Commonwealth and foreign air forces all over the world. It also has the Civil Aviation Authority's approval for use by aircrew in commercial aircraft. The combined lap and shoulder straps of the GQ harness are designed to restrict body movement when subjected to loads of up to 25G. For helicopters a 5-strap restraint harness prevents any involuntary forward, upward and lateral movement during flight and in the event of a crash landing. Since helicopters operate so frequently over water, each crewman sits on a personal survival pack which is incorporated in the harness and combines the benefits of comfort, correct ejection position and what GQ call 'crash survivability'. In plain English, the yellow plastic container, made in two hinged halves, contains a single-seat liferaft and a range of aids for survival on land and water. The container itself is made by the reinforced plastics unit set up by GQ in 1978 in a small factory leased from the Welsh Development Agency at Blackmill, near Bridgend, mainly to supply other companies in the Group—beginning with liferaft containers for RFD Inflatables.

Although GQ transferred their range of industrial safety equipment to Mills Equipment, they retained the manufacture of the GQ coverall, since it was regarded as an integral part of the parachutist's equipment. This garment had been specially designed for use by aircrew operating in tropical and temperate regions, and gives limited protection in the event of an aircraft flash fire.

It was only to be expected that many of the enthusiasts engaged in the revival of hot air ballooning in the early 1970s should turn to RFD for their equipment. Dagnall's early exploits with balloons and airships were still remembered, as well as the company's output of barrage balloons during the war and of parachute training balloons subsequently. The sport would have appealed enormously to Reg Dagnall (and indeed to Raymond Quilter) and it was therefore entirely in character that GQ Parachutes, to whom the job was delegated by the RFD Group, entered into the spirit of the movement regardless of the fact that there would never be much profit in it. And so it proved. The proponents of the hot air balloon would arrive at the factory with optimistic orders for twenty-five balloons at a time, hoping to sell one a week, but it usually soon dwindled to a virtually one-off business, with individual orders to meet special requirements of colour and wording. Nevertheless GQ are always happy to oblige, if only for old times' sake.

Protection from Danger

Military webbing equipment has continued to be the major product of Mills Equipment. But as well as personal load-carrying equipment, with modifications and additions specified by individual customers, Mills Equipment supply various webbing items—such things as slings and carrier cases—for use with weapons and armaments, and of course for tanks and aircraft.

The demand for ceremonial equipment has not diminished with the fragmentation of the British Empire—the newly independent countries are no less proud of their military parades. To meet this need, Mills Equipment supply white ceremonial equipment made of polyethylene webbing with brass, chrome-plated or nickel-plated fittings.

Meanwhile the company have also become the sole source of the industrial safety clothing and equipment which RFD have produced since the early post-war years. This has happened by degrees. At first, when Mills took on the safety equipment developed by GQ on joining the Group in 1969, RFD Inflatables continued to run their own industrial safety equipment business as they had done since the 1950s. This division of manufacture was perpetuated when RFD–GQ was formed in 1970 with separate Industrial Safety Equipment and Mills Equipment divisions, but two years later they were linked together in a single Industrial Safety and Mills Equipment division.

All this time Mills Equipment had been trading first as RFD and then as RFD–GQ, but on the disbandment of RFD–GQ in 1975 they became a separate manufacturing and trading subsidiary—RFD Mills Equipment Limited—within the Group for the first time. (In point of fact, the webbing equipment customers never stopped addressing themselves to Mills Equipment—the name was a part of their vocabulary—and the fact that their main contact, Len Oliver, was at the new location at Waterlooville meant that the company was still Mills Equipment as far as they were concerned.)

Since the war Mills Equipment had lost most of their aircrew safety harness business to GQ Parachutes, but during the 1950s they had built up a successful connection with the airlines in supplying passenger seat belts—British Overseas Airways being a principal customer. Then the airlines specified a new type of buckle which Mills found themselves unable to manufacture, and in the early 1960s the business went elsewhere, except for a few replacements ordered for aircraft equipped with the old-style belts.

The safety equipment inherited from GQ Parachutes when Mills Equipment moved into Waterlooville included the Paraguard stretcher, the harness-cum-clothing supplied mainly to the National Coal Board, and the general-purpose harness for people working at heights and in every condition where some form of suspension or restraint is required.

The Paraguard lightweight folding stretcher is a most versatile piece of equipment and is sold throughout the world to armed forces, fire brigades, ambulance services, industrial organisations, mining companies, shipping companies and airlines. It is invaluable in all kinds of emergencies, such as cliff and mountain rescues, because it is very light (22lb) and can be folded in half and packed in a valise which the rescuer can carry on his back. Provided the injured person does not have a damaged hip, the stretcher can be 'broken' in the centre to go round corners. The Paraguard is normally carried by four men but can be adapted for 2-man operation in restricted conditions. In helicopter rescues a 4-point lifting sling is used for raising or lowering the stretcher in a horizontal position, while V-straps are fitted at each end so that it can be raised or lowered in a vertical position in confined spaces or dragged along the floor or ground. At all times the patient is securely held on the stretcher by adjustable straps. RFD have every reason to be proud of the life-saving Paraguard, which has been designed and developed entirely by the Group with the collaboration of industrial medical officers.

The range of protective clothing made by Mills Equipment can cope with most kinds of industrial hazards. Here are some examples. The patented one-piece, gas-tight protection suit used in conjunction with breathing apparatus completely isolates the wearer from toxic atmosphere. Then there is the air-filled suit, which was taken up by the Associated Octel Company for use by operators clearing out sludge from tetra-ethyl lead blending tanks. For the blast furnacemen and rolling-mill operators of the British Steel Corporation the company produces clothing that can withstand molten slag and metal splash at approximately 1,400°C-1,600°C. An interesting point about this clothing is that the heavy fabric is 100 per cent pure wool made on the same principle as the melton material used for the traditional officer's greatcoat. For people in coke ovens and similar places the British Steel Corporation are supplied with all-wool gabardine jacket-and-trouser suits that repel water and resist flame.

For somewhat less arduous requirements, flame-resistant overalls and boiler-suits made of cotton drill and duck are provided. Finally, Mills Equipment fire-proximity clothing made of aluminised asbestos with internal linings of felt and nylon is worn by many official and company fire brigades, airfield crash-tender crews and motor-racing fire-fighting teams. Separate garments worn under the suit—as by racing drivers—can be made of flame-resistant Teklan.

The most popular type of headgear is the air-supplied plus-pressure mask which protects operators from toxic fumes and lead dust. The Harwell helmet, produced in collaboration with the UK Atomic Energy Authority to give protection against such hazards as liquid sodium and metallic sodium, is basically the same as the updraught helmet designed for use in opening up oil pipelines.

Smack on Target

Although RFD Systems Engineering contributed only a modest 9 per cent to the total group turnover in 1978 its products are by no means the least interesting. You have only to stand in a dome gunnery trainer with all systems going—the staccato bark of an anti-aircraft gun and the accompanying din of battle noises and low-flying aircraft as they zoom across the sky—to realise that you are witnessing a very exciting aspect of the RFD Group's activities.

The dome gunnery trainer is basically the same as the original Porta-bel described in Chapter Five. Later modifications to update the dome and its equipment resulted in some design problems calling for a rectification programme that was not completed until 1974. The current model is 40ft in diameter and accommodates a single gun mounting and its ancillary equipment, though a 60ft dome can be supplied if required and will take up to three guns. The dome is usually made of wood, with an external wooden cladding.

The trainer is designed to simulate attacks from single aircraft or groups of up to five aircraft flying in line astern. The aircraft appear as white silhouettes flying across the sky of the dome, as crossing targets flying at various speeds, approaching or receding targets flying at varying speeds, and as obliquely crossing targets. The images are strikingly realistic on their passage aross the sky and present the anti-aircraft gunner with 'live' targets for the most difficult part of his job—tracking. As every sportsman knows, an essential part of tracking a flying target is to fire at a point ahead of it, and this is provided for in the current dome trainer by a 'forward position spot' darting across the screen ahead of the aircraft.

The latest psychological equipment reproduces a variety of noises calculated to lessen the gunner's concentration—'mixed battle', 'aircraft', 'small arms', and 'shell fire'—individually or all at once with varying degrees of loudness.

After the war a refinement was added to the gunnery trainer for the benefit of naval anti-aircraft gunners in the form of a rolling platform for the gun mounting which reproduced the movement of the ship at sea.

The marksman trainer, which was a natural development of the dome trainer, was introduced in 1975–76 and has provided a valuable flow of orders from security forces of all kinds at home and abroad. It can be fitted up in any building with a suitably reinforced back-wall to prevent the pentration of .22 rim-fire ammunition. Its purpose is to train a man to fire a pistol accurately at targets projected on a screen, starting with cards, going on to static targets of the pop-up figure variety, and eventually moving targets in real-life scenes. The ordinary marksman trainer projects 35mm films on to a standard-size screen, while the advanced model is used with a wide Cinemascope screen.

As spin-off from the marksman trainer, RFD Systems Engineering became marketing agents for the pop-up targets produced by the Royal Ordnance factories. RFD Systems Engineering hold design authority for banner targets—originally called sleeve or flag targets—which have been produced by RFD since the early days of Reginald Dagnall.

Forward thinking in RFD Systems Engineering is perhaps less inhibited than elsewhere in the Group because the company is not so closely tied to a basic product as some of the other subsidiaries. Two projects currently being investigated are the Autotutor and a new form of training ammunition.

The Autotutor is an unprogrammed vehicle driving simulator which enables the learner driver to co-ordinate the controls and complete the first four hours of driver training in realistic conditions while in the safety of a building. This conforms with a growing belief among road safety authorities that initial driver training must be conducted off the highway. Indeed, several countries have already made the use of simulators mandatory in driver training.

The second project is an RFD invention called Tarp (training ammunition, re-useable plastic), which allows soldiers and others to practise firing their personal weapons indoors with only the same safety requirements as would be needed for air rifles. Tarp offers considerable potential savings in the cost of ammunition, transport, range booking and travel time.

Continuing Growth

Soon after Alan Craig and Peter Giles were appointed joint chief executives of RFD in the autumn of 1975, they suggested that the Group should purchase an interest in a firm called Lindsay & Williams, who specialised in the coating of textile tapes used in the manufacture of cables. The main object at that time was to provide a substantial outlet for woven nylon made by Perseverance Mill. A 28 per cent interest in the company was accordingly acquired and Peter Giles, who became a non-executive director on Craig's appointment as group managing director, moved up to Manchester to assume the role of chief executive of Lindsay & Williams.

It is of interest here to look back on Peter Giles's career up to this point. After leaving Nelson College, he went to Auckland University to read economics and accounting, but left after two years without graduating. He spent the next twelve months travelling around Europe and the Middle East before taking a job with a group of textile companies based on Manchester. Then he launched out in business on his own account as Peter Giles & Associates, advising private and public companies on acquisition and investment possibilities. Finally he teamed up with Alan Craig.

Under Giles's direction during the next three years Lindsay & Williams prospered. They bought a small company, J. W. & R. Healey, who had been in the rope, braid and twine business since the 1890s, and towards the end of 1978 acquired another small concern, Precision Coatings, to cater for the high-specification buoyancy-type fabrics used by RFD Inflatables.

In March 1979 Alan Craig left the RFD Group for personal reasons, having served it well as group managing director for four years. Peter Giles was appointed group managing director in his place, and the opportunity was taken to acquire the shares in Lindsay & Williams not previously held by the Group. Effective control was established in May, the total cost of the acquisition—£1 million—being provided by the Group's overdraft facilities.

WITH HINDSIGHT

Looking back on the history of the RFD Group, one can discern certain trends and characteristics that have influenced its development and perhaps draw some lessons for the future.

It has been, above all, a story of the steady improvement and updating of established products. All five of the main subsidiary companies are today making basically the same things as they were when they became a part of the Group—the inflatable dinghies which Reginald Foster Dagnall had experimented with even before he started his little RFD Company in 1920; the parachutes that Raymond Quilter and James Gregory designed and developed with such enthusiasm in the 1930s; the webbing equipment that Mills Equipment had been famous for since the Boer War; the top-quality textiles which Herbert Noble was beginning to make at about the same time; and the dome gunnery trainer which came on the scene during the Second World War.

But RFD have not rested on their laurels. Valuable additions to the Group's output have been introduced from time to time—the inflatable aircraft-recovery system and the inflatable escape chutes as supplied for Concorde, Perseverance Mill's superlative computer and typewriter ribbons, the protective suits for industry made by Mills Equipment, and Systems Engineering's marksman trainer.

The continuous improvement and development of RFD products over the years has created a tradition of design, quality and reliability that is the Group's most valuable asset. Indeed without that asset it could not have survived the crisis in 1973-74. It was the dedicated work of the designers, development engineers and workshop operatives —and the dependable performance of their products—that kept the Group afloat and enabled it to weather the storm. A company with products of lesser reputation would surely have foundered.

Even then, it took some time for the lesson to be fully appreciated, as Alan Craig, who was appointed group managing director after the crisis, admitted to the author: 'We had three phenomenal years to March 1977. We didn't realise it at the time but we had tremendously strong products. Throughout the Group we have very good products, and a lot of development work going into them.'

The recognition by top management of the vital importance of a company's products has been undermined in British industry in recent years by the widespread employment as chief executives and senior managers of accountants and others who lack practical industrial or commercial experience, and for whom managing a manufacturing business tends to become an exercise on paper. As one who had acquired that essential experience at an earlier stage, Peter Giles, the present Group chief executive, was able to identify how this trend has affected RFD:

> What struck me about the History as I read it is the extent to which the people who were running the company in the early days were involved in the products, what they were doing, and who they were making them for. I feel we have moved away from that involvement too far, and we've got to move back towards it.

But a change is on the way, as Peter Giles indicated: 'I see the essential part of my approach to be directly involved in what goes on in the business, so I spend plenty of time out and about, inside our factories, and with our major customers.'

Nevertheless, more remains to be done to bring the Group board in closer touch with the manufacturing companies, and it is therefore likely that the future evolution of the Group will be as lively and full of change as its past has been.

So far the RFD Group has avoided becoming an out-and-out conglomerate. There is an overall theme of safety and survival in most of the Group's products, just as there is a basic usage of textile fabrics. Nevertheless, there is a need for constant vigilance to guard against taking on new products that are outside the scope of the Group's present engineering skills, manufacturing capabilities, and marketing and management expertise.

All these are policy questions. When all is said and done, it is to the enthusiasm of the founders—Reginald Dagnall, Raymond Quilter, Herbert Noble—and their devoted followers, designing and making products that are still the best of their kind, that the Group owes its character and reputation, and will continue to look to for its inspiration in the future.

APPENDIX A

PRINCIPAL SUBSIDIARY COMPANIES OF THE RFD GROUP LIMITED

At 31st March, 1979

*Name and country of
incorporation and operation*   *Trading activities*

All subsidiaries are wholly owned except as otherwise indicated

United Kingdom

RFD Inflatables Limited	Manufacturers of marine and aircraft inflatable equipment and aircraft recovery systems
MFC Survival Limited	Manufacturers of inflatable products
GQ Parachutes Limited	Manufacturers of parachutes and ancillary equipment
RFD Mills Equipment Limited	Manufacturers of military webbing and industrial safety equipment
Mayday Equipment Limited	Manufacturers of military webbing and protective clothing
RFD Systems Engineering Limited	Manufacturers of military and civil gunnery training simulators
The Perseverance Mill Company Limited	Weavers of synthetic and fine cotton textiles
Albion Dyers & Finishers Limited	Textile dyers and finishers
Tranmere Textiles Limited	Processors of man-made fibres

Name and country of incorporation and operation	*Trading activities*

All subsidiaries are wholly owned except as otherwise indicated

Holland
RFD Holland BV — Manufacturers of marine and aircraft inflatable equipment

Australia
RFD Co. (Australia) Pty. Limited — Manufacturers of marine and aircraft inflatable equipment

Parachutes Pty. Limited — Suppliers of parachutes and ancillary equipment

U.S.A.
RFD-Patten, Inc. ((55% owned) — Manufacturers of marine and aircraft inflatable equipment

GQ Security Parachutes Inc. — Manufacturers of parachutes and ancillary equipment

APPENDIX B

RFD GROUP AND SUBSIDIARY COMPANIES
FINANCIAL RESULTS

(A) Summarised Results

Share Capital at 31 March 1979

	£
Authorised:	
100,000 3.85% Cumulative Preference Shares of £1	100,000
19,000,000 Ordinary Shares of 10p	1,900,000
Issued and fully paid:	
100,000 3.85% Cumulative Preference Shares of £1	100,000
13,630,290 Ordinary Shares of 10p	1,363,000
Total Reserves at 31 March 1979	10,259,000

Profits before tax from formation in 1936 to 1974

After achieving a net profit before tax of £15,722 in 1938 the RFD Company's profits dropped to an average of £8,000 during the war years and continued to decline afterwards until a loss of £1,856 was recorded in 1948. In the following year the company made a profit of £14,160 and thereafter went steadily forward to profits of £109,673 in 1954 and £200,979 in 1964. After reaching £505,642 in 1969, the Group's profits dipped to £464,037 in 1973 before plunging into a loss of £350,281 during the crisis of 1974. The subsequent progress of the Group is shown below.

Five Year Review

	1975 £000s	1976 £000s	1977 £000s	1978 £000s	1979 £000s
Turnover	11,621	14,710	15,970	18,745	21,401
Trading Profit	1,672	2,119	3,103	3,383	2,384
Interest (payable) receivable	(271)	(140)	56	68	(128)
Associated Company	—	—	—	48	60
Profit before tax	1,401	1,979	3,159	3,499	2,316
Taxation	193	1,036	1,691	1,089	435
Profit after tax	1,208	943	1,468	2,410	1,881
Minority interests	1	—	—	5	4
Extraordinary items and exchange gains (credit)	414	(87)	(44)	34	110
Preference dividend	4	4	4	4	4
Available for distribution	789	1,026	1,508	2,367	1,763
Ordinary dividend	161	175	195	217	368
Profit retained	628	851	1,313	2,150	1,395
Ordinary Shareholders' funds	5,348	6,145	7,576	9,726	12,109
Total funds employed	7,338	7,302	8,395	10,738	14,021
Earnings per share	8·82p	6·88p	10·74p	17·61p	13·74p
Ordinary dividend per share	1·18p	1·29p	1·43p	1·59p	2·70p
Dividend covered times	7·4	5·3	7·5	11·0	5·1
Net Assets per share	39p	45p	55p	71p	89p
Trading profit as a percentage of total funds employed	22·8%	29·0%	37·0%	31·5%	17·0%
Amount available for distribution as a percentage of Ordinary Shareholders' funds	14·7%	16·7%	19·9%	24·3%	1·45%

The figures for 1975 to 1977 have been re-stated in accordance with the Group's current accounting policies relating to the treatment of deferred tax and exchange differences.

(B) Analysis of Trading Activities, 1979

The analysis of turnover and trading profit of the principal activities before interest and taxation is:

	1979	
	Turnover	Profits
	£000s	£000s
Inflatable Products	8,979	888
Military Software and Industrial Safety Equipment	7,270	942
Specialist Textiles	5,152	554
	21,401	2,384

A geographical analysis of the trading of the Group is:

	1979	
	Turnover	Profits
	%	%
United Kingdom	82	107
Europe	7	(3)
Australia and U.S.A.	11	(4)
	100	100

Exports from the United Kingdom amounted to £4,813,000 in 1979.

ACKNOWLEDGMENTS AND
BIBLIOGRAPHY

This history could not have been written without a great deal of help from people in and outside the RFD Group—and from others who are now retired. My thanks are due to them all. It is impossible to mention more than a few by name—in any case many appear in the text—but there are some who deserve my special gratitude.

I particularly want to thank Mr Anton van Beugen Bik for giving me his first-hand account of events from the beginning of RFD as a public company to his retirement in 1973. Through all our conversations came the sense of leadership that he gave the company in its formative years as he carried on after Reginald Dagnall's death.

In trying to find out more about Dagnall as a person I managed to trace his nephew, Frank Martin, living in retirement at Farnham. This turned out to be a lucky stroke. Dagnall was childless, so he treated his young nephew almost like a son, with the result that Frank Martin was able to provide me with some fascinating photographs, papers and personal anecdotes of his famous uncle. I am indebted to him for the picture of Dagnall at the controls of the 'Bovril' airship in 1913.

Another great personality of the Group, Sir Raymond Quilter, was vividly recalled when Lady Quilter very kindly talked to me about him in her house in Suffolk. She could not have been more generous in drawing on her memories and supplying me with masses of photographs, without which I could not have done justice to her brilliant husband.

For the early story of GQ Parachute Company, my meeting with Arthur Dickinson was uniquely valuable.

The story of Mills Equipment up to 1956 was fully described in a privately published booklet written by Albert Lethern, who spent all his working life with the company, and I am grateful to Len Oliver for lending me his precious copy to draw upon. Supplementing Lethern's book, and enabling me to deal with the subsequent events up to the take-over by RFD in 1969, I was fortunate to be able to talk to Gerald

Fairlie, who served with Mills Equipment, first as works manager and latterly as a director, for nearly fifty years.

My research into the inflatables side of the Group was made all the easier by Betty Moat, the 'in-house' authority on the subject. Her own monograph, 'The contribution of liferafts to safety at sea', was an invaluable source of information, and she also made available to me the many documents she has collected dealing with the early years of Dagnall and his original company.

Since much of the RFD story is connected with aviation, I naturally spent many hours in the splendid library of the Royal Aeronautical Society benefiting from the help and advice of Arnold Nayler, the librarian, and his ever-willing assistant Michael Fitzgerald.

Finally, there is the overriding gratitude I owe to Mr David Mynors, the present Chairman of the Group, for his consistent encouragement. I have always found in these affairs that the continuous dialogue carried on between the author and his principal contact in the company is of critical importance. In the case of the RFD history this liaison could not have been more fruitful and sympathetic.

H.N.

The following are the principal works consulted in the preparation of this book. They are given in chronological order of publication.

British Airships, Past Present and Future, by George Whale, 1919
Airmen or Noahs, by Rear-Admiral Murray F. Sueter, CB., RN, 1928
Airships in Peace and War, by Michael Cumming and J. A. Sinclair, 1934
The Second World War, by Winston Churchill, 1948
Fifty Years of Brooklands, edited by Charles Gardner, 1956
The Development of the Mills Cartridge Belt, by Albert Lethern, 1956
Men and Machines, a history of D. Napier & Sons, by C. H. Wilson and W. J. Reader, 1958
Parachuting & Skydiving, by T. W. Willans, 1964
The Big Umbrella, by John Lucas, 1964
The Airships Akron and Macon, by Richard K. Smith, 1965
The Powerless Ones, Gliding in Peace and War, by Michael Cumming, 1966
British Gliders & Sailplanes, by Norman Ellison, 1971
Winston Churchill's Toyshop, by Stuart Macrae, 1971
The Father of British Airships—Ernest Willows, by Alec McKinty, 1972

INDEX